A Clean Place For My Fire

The story of Ivor and Rose Davies

Wayne Voss and Jeanette Knudsen

Publisher: DayStar Books Ltd

PO Box 65275,
Mairangi Bay,
Auckland 0754
New Zealand.

Cover Design: Outline Print Consultancy

Production: Outline Print Consultancy

Printed in New Zealand

ISBN: 978-1-99-115395-1

Psalm 24[1]

A Psalm of David

The earth is the Lord's, and all its fullness,
The world and those who dwell therein.
For He has founded it upon the seas, and es-
tablished it upon the waters.
Who may ascend into the hill of the Lord?
Or who may stand in His holy place?
He who has clean hands and a pure heart,
Who has not lifted up his soul to an idol, nor sworn deceitfully.
He shall receive blessing from the Lord,
And righteousness from the God of his salvation.
Such is the generation of those who seek him,
Who seek your face, God of Jacob.
Lift up your heads, O you gates!
And be lifted up, you everlasting doors!
And the King of glory shall come in.
Who is this King of glory?
The Lord strong and mighty, The Lord mighty in battle.
Lift up your heads, O you gates! Lift up, you everlasting doors!
And the King of glory shall come in.
Who is this King of glory?
The Lord of hosts, He is the King of glory.

[1] This was one of Ivor Davies's favourite scriptures which he often read
and spoke about before he told the story of the Congo revival.

Endorsements

A Clean Place for My Fire is the challenging and inspiring story of early missionary exploits in the Belgian Congo. The reader cannot help but be moved to action by the commitment, dedication, sacrifice, and faith as evidenced through the lives and ministry of Ivor and Rose Davies.

In the pages of this book is a message portraying the power of confession, repentance and forgiveness as precursors for the unity where God commands the blessing in revival. We along with many others have been deeply challenged through the Davies' ministry, resulting for ourselves a lifetime in missions.

Dr. Bruce and Barbara Thompson
College of Counselling and Health Care
University of the Nations

I met Ivor and Rose in 1979, having heard of the story of the remarkable East African Revival and its influence on the Congo and beyond. To me that was one of the purest and beautiful revivals in recent history. In my early years in Africa I met up with many Africans who had been converted through that revival.

Ivor and Rose's life and ministry has been a blessing to many around the world – not least in New Zealand and they have deeply impacted us all in WEC. I look forward eagerly to reading this book about the life and ministry of Ivor and Rose. My prayer is that this book may stir all who read it to trust God for further outpourings of God's Spirit in today's world.

Patrick Johnstone
WEC International – UK
Author Emeritus of Operation World

A Clean Place for My Fire will both challenge and bless you. Acts 4 13 says, "...the disciples were unschooled, ordinary men....that had been with Jesus." Ivor and Rose Davies were also very much ordinary people who were in love with Jesus, following Him to the Congo and to the ends of the earth, New Zealand.

Their journey of faith will inspire you and you will get caught up in their adventure of faith of how God moved and answered prayer. You will be challenged as you read of the revival in Africa and the later suffering of Congolese believers and missionaries during the Simba rebellion, many of whom were martyred. You will also be blessed to know that God wants to use you as He used them.

It was a privilege to have known Ivor and Rose and to have learned from them the joys and challenges of adjusting and living in another culture.

Doug Plummer
Former WEC Taiwan Field leader
Former Jian Hua Foundation Executive Director

Contents

Preface

Ivor Davies believed the events of 1953 in the Belgian Congo were most significant and it is now clear that his appraisal was correct. The lives of many thousands of Congolese were dramatically affected by what took place. Later, countless Christians throughout the world were transformed as a result of Ivor's reports and public addresses. Audiences sat in stunned silence after Ivor recounted what became known as the 'Congo Revival'.

Though God had his hand on Ivor from birth, his experiences in 1953 proved to be the pivotal point of his life. He and Rose were centre stage as the amazing drama unfolded. But there is more to tell than just the events of 1953. This is their story, the story of Ivor and Rose Davies, Welshman and English woman, missionaries, participants and eye witnesses to the Belgian Congo revival of the 1950s.

The original manuscript was written in the 1990s by former journalist Wayne Voss who felt he should record the significant narrative of Ivor and Rose's life. Wayne had attended Valley Road Baptist Church and was among the large gathering at Ivor's memorial service after he passed away. Realising that someone should document Ivor and Rose's story, Wayne approached Megan Davies, who gave her permission and handed over a large box of family letters, audio tapes and photos.

Ivor and Rose had been prolific letter writers, often writing daily to their children and wider family in Britain, even though they lived in the remotest corner of Africa. Wayne researched the correspondence, interviewed family members and visited Ivor's brother David in Wales, seeing first-hand the Welsh environment in which Ivor was raised.

The resulting script lay unpublished for some decades until John Watson, a WEC (Worldwide Evangelisation for Christ) missionary to Thailand with his wife Alison, suggested to his sister, Jeanette Knudsen, that she might like to construct it into a book.

Jeanette met with Ivor and Rose's youngest daughters, Megan Davies, a retired nurse, and Ruth Charman and her husband Maurice, former WEC missionaries, and together they agreed that the manuscript should be resurrected. It was time for the story of missions and revival to be presented to a modern audience.

Though these noteworthy events took place over 70 years ago they are still relevant today, calling us to renew our commitment to the Lord, to respond to the high calling of missionary endeavour and to pray for revival in the 21st century

Wayne Voss
Jeanette Knudsen

June 2023

Foreword

When I read the manuscript of the biography of my brother, Ivor, the Bible story of Joseph and his 'coat of many colours' flashed through my mind. The authors have succeeded in presenting the 'many colours' of Ivor's life. There is something for everybody: for the seeker who wants to know how to be reconciled with God and to obtain assurance of eternal salvation; for the disciple who seeks enlightenment about the problem of guidance; about sacrifice for Jesus' sake; about the call of God to service; about the founding of churches where no church existed; and about the powerful and mysterious workings of the Holy Spirit in a mighty revival. And one thing more – God can call, equip and use in an outstanding manner any person that is surrendered to His will.

Perhaps Ivor will be remembered most of all for his involvement in the 1953 revival which swept through the north-east of the Belgian Congo. Ivor later travelled widely, reporting on those days. As a result of his ministry, many people were revived in their devotion to the Saviour and in their relationship with fellow believers.

Some were puzzled about the strange phenomena Ivor spoke of. I can sympathise with them; revival days are unusual days, and unusual things occur. My wife and I, together with other missionaries, ministered at Wamba during that time, a distance of 260 kilometres from Ivor's area. We also witnessed strange phenomena, but not as much or as varied as Ivor saw at Opienge.

We tested the occurrences by three rules:

- Were there similar phenomena found in Holy Scripture?

- Did they bear the fruit of the Spirit, like love, joy, and peace?

- Was there evidence of the exalting of the person and work of our Lord Jesus Christ?

The fulfilling of the third test, in particular, gave us great satisfaction. Shall we ever forget the reverence, love and joy offered to Jesus as the people sang in Swahili, "I was a prodigal, lost in sin . . . ," and then the chorus, sung with such deep feeling and praise, "How I praise His name – Jesus; He died there on Calvary, to take away my sin."

The marks of that heavenly visitation remain to this day on people's lives. The phenomena passed, but what God did abides.

David Davies, brother of Ivor Davies

31 March 1995, Wales

1

A Clean Place for My Fire

Into the gathering of a group of Congolese Christians walked a stranger. He strode to the front and began speaking about sin, about polygamy and other wrong doings. The hearts of his listeners flooded with conviction as they digested his words. They started to cry with deep sobs and to tremble violently, begging God for forgiveness. The speaker then mysteriously disappeared. It was February 1953, in a small village near the Lubutu mission station, in one of the remotest corners of the Heart of Africa Mission area in the Belgian Congo.

The six Lubutu missionaries heard of the event and responded by sending two of their number to the village to investigate. As a result, village pastors and their wives were invited to the mission station for a 10-day conference. The missionaries were concerned about what had taken place and felt the leaders needed further teaching on the work of the Holy Spirit. One missionary each day arranged to address the 40 pastors on related topics.

One morning the address was based on Acts 19, where the apostle Paul asked the men of Ephesus if they had received the Holy Spirit; they replied that they had not even heard there was a Holy Spirit. That evening, while the missionaries were holding their own prayer meeting, the pastors congregated in the school house, discussing the message delivered earlier. Its impact caused them to question whether they, like the men of Ephesus, had the anointing of the Holy Spirit. Unlike the Ephesians, they acknowledged, they did not have the apostle Paul to lay hands on them.

"Why don't we ask one of the missionaries to come and lay hands on us?" one pastor suggested. Others argued that such a request was pointless, as the missionaries had never done anything like that before, talking about such things, but never actually doing them.

"What are we going to do then? What's going to happen to us without the power of the Holy Spirit?" another pastor asked, looking at the fearful faces around him.

One of the men stood up and cried out, "Oh Lord, please help us!"

Immediately the Holy Spirit fell on the group. The scene was astonishing. Some were pushed over by what they later described as a powerful wind, throwing them off their feet and sending them crashing over seats. Some cried out in agony, while others stood with raised arms, loudly rejoicing and praising God. Most experienced violent trembling and shaking, as if they were electrocuted by an unseen source.

The missionaries nearby heard the uproar and rushed into the school house to discover what was wrong. They were aghast at the scene that confronted them, going from person to person, attempting to calm them down. But to no avail. Some of the pastors were caught up worshipping God in a way they had not witnessed before. Others, standing, kneeling, or lying prostrate on the floor, struggled to confess hidden sin to an unseen person.

They ignored all attempts to close the meeting, and the missionaries resigned themselves to remain spectators of the remarkable events. After two hours the Spirit seemed to lift, allowing the pastors to compose themselves. They looked around at each other in amazement. Despite the fact that some had been thrown bodily about the room by an invisible force, no one was injured.

At a loss as to what to do or say, the missionaries encouraged them to retire to their sleeping quarters. The exhausted men slowly dispersed from the school house to join their families, trying to comprehend what they had just experienced. But if they thought it was over they were confronted with another surprise. The pastors had barely entered their accommodation when the Holy Spirit fell on their wives and children. The women began to shake, cry, sing or pray. Children climbed out of bed to confess stealing to their parents and to ask for forgiveness. The missionaries found sleep impossible, for they were awakened by people desperate to confess their pilfering, as if their very lives depended upon immediate confession.

The next day the confessions continued. Children went crying to their teachers to ask for forgiveness for stealing from classrooms. Labourers arriving to work at the mission were immediately convicted of sin as they stepped onto the station compound. Christian and non-Christian alike were thrown to the ground until they confessed their sins. Then they sensed a joy and freedom, such as they had not known before, and they began noisily praising God.

The missionaries were dumbfounded. They had prayed for revival but had not expected anything like what they were now witnessing. They wrote letters to the other stations, reporting the astonishing events, including one to Ivor Davies in Opienge. He read aloud the account to his fellow missionaries – his wife Rose, Sarah Ross, and Aubrey and Hulda Brown, two new arrivals.

What did they think, he asked them. They represented a mixed group of church backgrounds – Anglican, Mennonite, Methodist, Presbyterian and Baptist – but they had little idea of what had happened. Perhaps the events were inspired by too much emotion and fear. They were particularly worried by what people in Britain would think if they heard about the Lubutu events. They decided to continue their regular fasting and prayer on the third Thursday of each month. In reality, they acknowledged later, their prayers became conditional; they wanted revival, but not the Lubutu experience.

Ivor and Aubrey departed on a 200-kilometre trek to preach in villages in the Opienge region. After two weeks they came to the final village on their itinerary, about 40 kilometres from Opienge. That evening as they settled into their accommodation, they heard outside the footsteps of a runner from Opienge bringing letters from their wives. Ivor sat at the table with Rose's letter, while Aubrey relaxed in the corner of the room with his wife's message. As Ivor read the letter, he grew increasingly horrified, breaking out in a hot and cold sweat.

Rose described how Sena, wife of Lubutu elder, Farusi, arrived at Opienge in May 1953 to visit her mother, having walked 200 kilometres. Her purpose was to seek her forgiveness for her previous resentful attitude. On Sunday, several days later, Sena attended a service in the hall. While Rose was speaking, people noticed that Sena's body began to jerk and shake in an unusual manner. One or two approached her wishing to help her, thinking she was unwell, but she told them she was not ill; rather the Holy Spirit had poured his anointing on her. Some were astonished and others amused.

The following Tuesday night, Peleza, wife of Matalembo, the chief Opienge elder, woke up their neighbours with loud singing, hallelujahs, and praises to God. People flocked to her house and found her on her bed sitting upright and shaking violently.

"Asenti," she shouted, "asenti, asenti, Bwana Yesu!" – thanks, thanks, thanks, Lord Jesus! Some declared she had gone insane, while others thought she was physically ill. As she quietened down, people returned to their homes.

However at 4.00 am she woke them again with the same behaviour, singing in Congo-Swahili, "Kuna nuru moyoni mwangu" – there is a light in my heart. She told people she had seen a light that came closer and closer to her until it burst on her and filled her heart. Some were speechless, while some laughed and said she had "gone off her top". Others rebuked them, saying it was better to wait and see if it was the Lord's doing.

The next morning Peleza told Rose that she had a vision from the Lord in the night where she saw a bright light and heard a voice.

"Peleza," the voice said, "I want to do a great work here at Opienge, but there is much hardness. If you want to light a good fire, do you get one by laying the wood among the ashes?"

"No," Peleza answered.

"What must be done then?" the voice asked.

"Clean away the ashes first," Peleza said.

The voice replied, "That is right, and I want a clean place for my fire. Tell the people that those who have a bag of sin hidden away in their hearts are to open it up and make confession, so that the Lord can do a great work in them."

The following Sunday, Sarah Ross was taking the service when the Spirit again came on Peleza, much to the amazement of the people. She began to pray loudly and praise God at the rear of the hall, drowning out Sarah's attempts to conduct the service. Some told her to be still, but to no avail. In desperation Sarah turned to Rose for help. Rose told Peleza she had to be quiet so that God's Word could be preached. When the appeals failed to have any effect, she was shuffled outside, where she continued her noisy praise. Sarah attempted to proceed with her sermon but it was impossible, for Peleza's voice penetrated the walls of the building, and the meeting was abandoned.

The more Ivor read of the events in Rose's letter, the greater his fear grew.

Little did Ivor know that he was about to step out on the greatest experience of his whole life.

2

Boyhood in Wales

The thin, pallid twelve-year-old boy lay weak and exhausted on his bed, a picture of misery and distress, wracked by coughing and laboured breathing. Little seemed to stand between him and an early grave. In spite of the love, care and attention that his family lavished on him, the lung infection continued to inflict its terrible toll. When his parents, Evan and Mary Davies, realised that the boy was suffering from life- threatening double pneumonia, with both lungs affected, they shifted out of their bedroom so that their son, Ivor, could be better cared for in their double bed.

The year was 1916, well before the age of penicillin and antibiotics. The family lived in their modest cottage of Ryecroft, built by Ivor's father and two uncles, in the small village of Gowerton, six miles[1] northwest of Swansea, near the south coast of Wales. In the small crowded home accommodating two adults and seven children, no one could escape the sound of Ivor's wheezing that continued day and night.

His parents placed hot antiphlogistine poultices on his sides in an attempt to reduce the pain and inflammation. To cool his fever, his mother soaked brown paper bags in cold vinegar and laid them on his forehead. At times he was delirious, imagining weird and wild apparitions when he stared in the long mirror on the wardrobe door. His family and other visitors presented a passing pageant of long sad faces as they called by to check on him.

As he began to improve, family members carefully and lovingly carried him downstairs in the evenings to sit with them around the fire. His eldest sister, Olwen, was his mother's constant helper, carrying him to a chair she placed outside, as he gained strength. She fussed around, ensuring that he enjoyed the fresh air and sunshine, later carrying him back inside. Because he had lost such a lot of weight and was so weak, people did not expect him to survive, certainly thinking him too frail to finish school.

But Ivor, the third of the seven children, did recover.

Nevertheless, the detrimental effects of the illness on his health and confidence were obvious for years afterwards. The traumatic experience left a permanent imprint on his mind, causing him to be nervous and unsure of himself. He grew shy and introverted, and his peers often teased him because of his attachment to home.

The six-month interruption to his studies topped a series of events that seriously marred his formal education. School was a struggle. He loved the happy times of his kindergarten days but when he moved to primary school he failed the examination and was kept back in the same class of standard one for an extra year. It distressed him that others of his age moved on ahead of him.

At standard two level, the cycle of exam failure and retention in the same class for another year was repeated. The experience affected his entire school life. He disliked school, believing that his teachers misunderstood him or his feelings. He lost all desire to do well and looked for any reason to avoid attending school, often feigning sickness. By the time Ivor reached the school-leaving age of fourteen he departed, having failed to complete all the standards.

Ivor's parents were Welsh Presbyterians who endeavoured to instil strict Christian principles in their children. The family attended the local fellowship and the children regularly went to Sunday school. At home the family spoke in Welsh, with singing an important part of their lives. Their father Evan was a choir conductor and the whole family sang, taking solo parts in musical presentations like Handel's Messiah.

Ivor was born on 21st August 1904, the same year that Wales first experienced the Welsh Revival, a significant wave of spiritual resurgence. It was a period of tremendous religious fervour, when the Holy Spirit brought many to repentance and conversion. As Ivor grew up, the local churches were full of people who had lived through the event, and he heard numerous accounts of what had taken place.

Less than two miles from Gowerton was the home of the renowned Welsh revivalist, Evan Roberts, one of the revival leaders. Though he was the best known, it would be misleading to believe that the revival started with him or even depended on his direction. It spread, Eifion Evans wrote, with no advertisements, no brass bands, no posters, no huge tents, no organisation and no overall director.[2] According to James Stewart, it was a revival of young people and of singing, a revival of prayer and of soul-winning, and a revival of personal experience, all under the control of the Holy Spirit.[3]

As a result of the extraordinary revival, a remarkable transformation took place in the community, which by the turn of the century had been experiencing rapid moral decay. New converts in their tens of thousands packed Welsh churches, emptying public bars of patrons. The high incidence of drunkenness and other crime dramatically declined, virtually placing the police force out of work. Football matches were cancelled because players and spectators were elsewhere taking part in revival meetings.

Many of the new converts were coal miners, who held services underground during their lunch breaks. Pit-ponies in some mines no longer understood the miners' instructions because of the sudden absence of oaths and curses. Wives and husbands, parents and children, and people at enmity with each other were reconciled, and churches of different denominations settled their differences. People repaid debts with money that once would have been spent on alcohol and gambling, and workers turned up for work on time.

Many came from around the world to Wales to witness events first hand and they became catalysts for other mini-revivals on their return to their homelands or areas of mission.[4]

However, revival stories and his parent's faith were insufficient to make Christianity a reality for Ivor. He found it a formal and remote experience. He knew his father as a deeply religious man, but though he conducted church choirs he did not pray audibly or read the scriptures with his family. His mother Mary prayed only with the younger children. Ivor attended church and eventually became a Sunday school superintendent, but he did not respond to invitations during meetings to accept Christ as his personal Saviour.

In the year following Ivor's exit from school, his father found him several successive jobs, including placements on a farm and in a timber factory. But Ivor's acute shyness and lack of commitment worked against him. Few of his jobs lasted long; in one placement, he remained for just two days.

One night when Ivor came home late after the family had gone to bed, as he had fallen into the habit of doing, he overheard a conversation. As he crept upstairs and passed his parents' door, he heard them talking, and to his amazement, he realised they were discussing himself.

"I don't know what is to become of him. We've tried our best but he doesn't listen to anything we say. It looks like he's going to become a ne'er-do-well," he heard his father say.

The word 'ne'er-do-well' shocked Ivor. It dawned on him just how poor was his parents' estimation of him. His father had previously used the term 'ne'er-do-well' in reference to a local personality who lived in a shack in a wood near their home; the man did not work but lived off what he scavenged or what people gave him. Ivor went into his room and lay down on his bed, wide awake, his thoughts in a turmoil.

"I'll never be like that, I'll never be like that!" he repeated to himself. He determined that any new job his father got for him he would stick at, even if he hated it. He would work hard and prove that he was able to earn his living. He would not be a disgrace to his parents.

The incident on the stairway was a catalyst, shaking him into understanding what life was about – a person had to be responsible for giving all their heart and energy to what was before them. His next job involved an apprenticeship with a painter and decorator, the training of which took five years to complete. Although he detested the smell of paint he persevered, becoming a skilled craftsman. From the experience Ivor developed a strong sense of stability and persistence, something he never lost.

In 1925, when Ivor was 21 years old, his father died after a long illness. Part of the responsibility for supporting the family fell on Ivor's shoulders. Since the country was in the grip of the 1920s' depression they were difficult years for working class families like the Davies, when they could barely earn enough money on which to survive.

Added to Ivor's problems was an intense inner personal crisis.

[1] Miles used for distances in the UK, kilometres in the rest of the world.

[2] Eifion Evans, *The Welsh Revival of 1904*, page 166.

[3] James Stewart, *Invasion of Wales by the Spirit through Evan Roberts*, pages 15-17.

[4] For more information on the revival, see www.moriahchapel.org.uk

3

Make Yourself Real to Me

Ivor's heart and mind was a battle ground. He recognised he was a hypocrite, outwardly appearing to belong to the Lord, but inwardly a needy sinner. He told people he was a Christian but he knew in his heart he was not. His awareness of his double life tormented and frustrated him and in his spirit he felt weighed down by a heavy load, robbed of joy and peace.

His Christian parents brought up their children to fear God. He knew it was wrong to lie, yet he told untruths, like lying to his mother about where he had been. He knew it was wrong to steal, yet he stole from his employer. Conviction and turmoil disturbed him day and night and he became deeply unhappy. He prayed, repeating prayers his mother had taught him as a child, but the words seemed hollow and he received no answers. God was not real.

When inner frustration and dissatisfaction became too much to bear Ivor retreated to the isolation of the countryside to be alone and to sing. He loved singing, a delight he inherited from his choir-master father who spent many hours teaching his children to sing. Alone, Ivor whiled away his hours, singing loudly and melodically to himself and enjoying relief from his inner struggles.

At the same time he was going steady with Lilian, a fine Christian young woman, with whom he had been friends for some time. He regularly visited her parents' home and they treated him like a member of the family. One evening he called at her parents' home to meet her when they were eating their evening meal. He reached the dining room door and had his hand on the knob when he heard her father praying with the family. As he waited outside for him to finish, Ivor realized Lilian's father was praying for himself, pleading with the Lord for his salvation. He was filled with an overwhelming sense of conviction. For the next few weeks he was in turmoil, losing all sense of peace.

Another evening, weeks later, he arrived at their home just as they were going out. They told him their daughter, a nurse, was not home yet, as her employers had asked her to work several hours longer. Although they were going out, they told him he was welcome to stay and wait for her. He sat down in front of the fire in the lounge and tried to read but his mind and heart were in confusion. He recalled the prayer Lilian's father had prayed and the revelation then in his heart that he was not living as God wished.

What am I going to do, he thought with despondency. He raised up his arms and called out, "Oh God, if you are real, make yourself real to me!" Then, as if to underline his earnest prayer, he stretched himself out full length on the floor. In desperation he lay there, waiting for what seemed a long time, but nothing happened.

There you are, a fellow nearly six feet tall throwing yourself down on the floor. What a fool you are, he thought and he got up. Then he pondered his actions again.

"No", he said to himself, "I meant it. Lord, I've spoken to you – I want you to make yourself real to me. If you're God, make yourself real to me!" Lilian came home and they went out together, but he said nothing to her about his prayer.

The following morning Ivor rode off to work on his cycle, taking his normal route from Gowerton to the neighbouring village along a country lane bounded by frosty fields. As a typical Welsh man, he sang at the top of his voice the hymns he had been brought up with, improvising on tenor and bass. The cows and sheep in the adjacent fields were his only audience.

As usual, he sang in Welsh, without listening to the words, for it was the tune and the harmonies that he loved. Suddenly the reality of the words burst on to his consciousness:

Dyma gariad fel y moroedd,
Tosturiaethau fel y lli:
Twysog Bywyd pur yn marw –
Marw i brynu'n bywyd ni.

Here is love vast as the ocean,
Loving kindness as a flood,
When the prince of life our ransom,
Shed for us His precious blood.

Who his love will not remember,
Who can cease to sing His praise?
He can never be forgotten,
Throughout heavn's eternal days.

On the mount of crucifixion,
Fountains opened deep and wide,
Through the floodgates of God's mercy,
Flowed a vast and gracious tide.

What beautiful words! He always sang them as a matter of course, without really listening to them. As he rode he began to register the meaning of the words. They were about the blood of Christ and about the Cross. He searched in his mind and heart to understand the message, realising there was a reality in them that he had totally ignored before. At work he continued to sing and by lunchtime his work mates started to notice.

"Hello, who have we here? Have we got a preacher today?" they said, making fun of him. When they asked him why he was singing all the day he replied, "Well, it's such a fine beautiful day today." In fact it was raining.

When he rode home the same thing happened. He sang all the way, and as he reached his village, he knew what was taking place. He believed the words; they were full of meaning and he understood them. "I'm saved!" he said in amazement. Then he was aware of a voice, not audible, but in his heart.

"Didn't you fall down on the ground last night and ask me that, if I was real, I should indeed make myself real to you?"

"Yes Lord," he replied, "you've made yourself real to me in these hymns I know so well." As the revelation came, joy flooded his heart. God had answered his prayer.

Then he got a shock, for the Lord issued him a challenge. "Now I've made myself real to you, go home and tell the family tonight."

The Davies was a close-knit family who enjoyed each other's company. In the evenings they exchanged accounts of the day's events over the dinner table, then after the meal, they settled down around the fire and shared stories. When Ivor arrived home from work that evening, in January 1928, the challenge to share his special news weighed heavily on his mind, for he did not believe word of his conversion would be well received.

The Lord wants me to tell the family, but I'll wait until after the meal, he thought. When the meal finished and his sister began a story he decided to wait until she had finished. Then she started another one and he resolved to wait until she had concluded that one. The same pattern continued all evening and eventually everyone went to bed.

The next day, on his cycle again, he started singing but the desire to sing faded out and he realised there was a problem. In not telling the family about his salvation he had failed to do what the Lord asked of him.

I've failed him, he repeated to himself. He did not sing at work that day. As he rode home he said to himself, *I will tell them! I must to do it tonight.*

After the meal, when they were all sitting around the table, he saw his sister primed up to share her latest story.

"I've got something to say. I'm saved!" he blurted out, just as she launched into her narrative. Silence filled the room, broken only by the ticking of the kitchen clock.

"What did you want to say that for?" someone said.

"Because I mean it, I really mean it," he replied,

"Oh, you've spoiled the evening," Olwen exclaimed and stormed off to her bedroom. One after another three of his siblings departed to bed, leaving his mother, his youngest brother, David, and himself. His mother, her head bowed, was quiet and his brother sat there, staring at him.

What'll I do, what'll I say? Have I said something to hurt my mother, Ivor thought.

They continued to sit in silence. Then his mother raised her head.

"My son," she said, "I know what you're saying. When I was 21 years old, I did what you did and I invited God into my life. I went on well with the Lord. When I got married and you children came along, however, I slackened off. I didn't pray regularly and I didn't read the Word as I should have." She paused and looked down at her hands. Then she spoke again. "What you've said tonight has really touched me. My backsliding is over."

Immediately she knelt down at her chair and, in a quiet halting voice, gave her heart back to the Lord. Six months later David, aged seventeen, made the decision to follow the Lord and in time, Ivor's other surviving brothers and sisters did as well.

Ivor later wrote of his conversion: "The Lord graciously bent down and accepted this unworthy and sinful soul of mine in the month of January of the year 1928. For the wonderful and unexplainable gift of life eternal, I mean to give Him all I have and all I am, that he might use me for His glorification. I mean to do this in deed as well as in word. Praise ye the Lord." He signed it: Ivor Davies, Ryecroft, Gorwydd Road, Gowerton, Wales.

Later, Ivor and his brother David held open-air meetings in their village. Their action annoyed some of their chapel friends who did not regard such gatherings as appropriate aspects of church life. Others found it strange that an individual as introverted and shy as Ivor should hold a public street meeting in front of his own community, little understanding it was his new-found confidence and faith in God that gave him the boldness he had not previously possessed.

4

Bible College Student

Ivor shuffled from foot to foot as he stood in front of his distraught mother.

"And how do you think we are going survive as a family without your income?" she questioned him, her voice heavy with accusation through her tears.

For several months, after his revelation of salvation, Ivor continued to work as a painter and decorator. As the eldest son still at home with his mother it was his responsibility to be the family's chief breadwinner. The area of Wales where the family lived suffered badly from the effects of the world-wide economic depression, with one coal mine after another closing and thousands of men losing their jobs. Ivor was still employed and each week gave his mother most of his earnings for the household expenses, retaining only a little pocket money for himself.

Later in 1928 Ivor sensed God was prompting him to enter full time Christian service. He was particularly impressed by Scottish pioneer, John G. Paton's book, *Missionary to the New Hebrides*, concerning South Pacific evangelism. However, it was a line from Shakespeare's *Julius Caesar* which spoke most clearly to him: *There is a tide in the affairs of men which, taken at the flood, leads on to fortune.*[1]

Ivor felt the Lord brought the words to his mind and he clearly understood the message. He did not need a prophet or church leader to explain to him what God was telling him. There was a flood before him and it was time for him to launch out. If he jumped into action it would lead to success. As he meditated on it, the Lord spoke to him about reaching out to others for their salvation. In response he yielded himself to God and his service, wherever the Lord led.

The first difficulty was to tell his mother he had decided to become a missionary. He was sure she would be disturbed by his decision, for he was the family breadwinner and they all relied on his wages. As he expected, she dissolved into tears.

"Don't cry, mother, don't cry," Ivor stammered as she started to list the things they needed money for, like shoes for his sister and repairs to the roof, as well as the day-to-day necessities.

As she grew more upset Ivor stumbled, "I can see my responsibility at home. I'll stay, don't worry, I'll stay." For the next few days he felt very uneasy in his spirit.

"Lord, I'm willing to go," he kept crying out within, "but what are you going to do about the situation at home?"

Unbeknown to Ivor, Mary, his mother, later went to her room to pray. She felt the Lord ask her why she had cried in response to her son's statement. Then he brought to her mind an incident from over 22 years ago, when she was pregnant with Ivor. He reminded her how she had knelt at her bedside and dedicated the child, boy or girl, to him. She wanted the baby she was carrying to be his and to be used for whatever service he had in store. The Lord then asked her if she thought he had accepted her vow.

"Yes, Lord," she replied.

"Are you ready now to give him over to my service?" he questioned.

"Yes, Lord," she replied again.

Two days later she surprised Ivor with her change of heart, sharing with him the story of her pregnancy and her dedication of her unborn baby.

"So I'm not holding you back any longer. I believe the Lord will take care of things for me and the family[2]," she said. "I am at peace with your proposal and you are free to go."

Despite her words Ivor felt he still had a responsibility to his mother to support the family. What he did not know was that his job was about to come to an end. Two weeks later the depression took its toll on Ivor's employer's business and there was insufficient work for him. As an unemployed person he had to wait a month following registration before he could claim unemployment benefits. The first week without pay passed, the second, and then the third, with Ivor eating and sleeping in the household but unable to contribute anything.

"What are you doing?" the Lord seemed to say to him. Ivor knew what he meant and responded that he was supporting his mother.

"Are you really?" the reply came. "You're not giving anything to your mother like your brothers and sisters. Haven't I called you into full-time service? Your mother has taken her hands off you, so why don't you move?"

The battle within him continued, even after he received his first unemployment benefit. Finally he braved the subject with his mother again and she assured him that though he was no longer earning the Lord was looking after them. Ivor knew he had to make a move. He found work again, enabling him to give money to his mother, but he knew it was only until he went to Bible college.

Ivor had occasionally attended evening services at the Bible College of Wales in Swansea, just five miles from his home. It opened four years earlier in 1924 by Rees Howells.[3] Ivor sensed the Lord's prompting to speak to him about the possibility of applying to become a full time student. Though it usually took two months for applications to be processed, Rees Howells invited him to start straight away, telling him he had been watching him and was pleased he had approached him.

Any heady notions Ivor held concerning full time service for the Lord came crashing down when he began his studies. He had led a physically active outdoor life as a house decorator and that, coupled with his disastrous school background, made his four years of student life very difficult. He was not accustomed to sitting on a hard seat all day listening to lengthy, mentally demanding lectures and struggling to concentrate.

Several times during the first six months he thought of packing his bags and running. During one point of despondency he went to God in prayer, protesting resentfully about his lot. But he sensed the Lord telling him to relax and be assured that he was in the right place. All Ivor had to do was to give himself to the Lord who would enable him to succeed. Gradually Ivor coped with the long hours of concentration and study, comprehending that the Lord knew his potential better than he himself did.

Another major personal struggle concerned the need to submit to the authority of the college. He found there were rules and regulations about everything from those in authority and he discovered he did not want to follow every little detail. Before long he became aware of a section of the student body who thought like himself. They formed a noticeable enclave, divorcing themselves from the main body and getting together to discuss what they perceived as unnecessary protocols.

"Get away from that group," Ivor felt the Lord say to him. "Be willing to do whatever the authorities tell you to do. Are you willing for that?" He struggled with the issue, as there were some things he really did not like.

"Yes, Lord," he said in eventual submission, "I believe you knew all about this place before I came here and still you directed me here. You want me to agree to what is happening here." Finding a new freedom he noticed that he concentrated better without being sidetracked by other issues, and he began to benefit from the teaching he received.

In Ivor's last year of study his younger brother David[4] followed him to the college and they shared a makeshift room above the lecture hall. They grew close together and experienced regular times of joint prayer.

Ivor often prayed concerning his future location of missionary work. But no direction came. He was sure he was called to missionary work but whenever he asked where it was or what mission society he should go with there was only silence.

Frequent addresses at the college by missionaries working in various parts of the world failed to point Ivor in any particular direction. The only helpful words were those concerning the need to wait, like the words of Habakkuk 2. 3: 'For the revelation awaits an appointed time; it speaks of the end and will not prove false. Though it linger, wait for it; it will certainly come and will not delay.'

It seemed reasonable to pray for his future place of service and to write to people there to find out information, but he knew he must trust the Lord and learn the key lessons before him. When he was asked to give an address at the beginning of the term he would tell how the Lord called him into his service and how he was waiting for God's direction for his next step. Waiting was certainly an issue on which he could speak from experience.

The life of faith, the ability to trust God for everything, and the life of prayer were major themes of the Bible College of Wales and of Rees Howells, who often led the students for daily prayers. Sometimes he announced that lectures would be cancelled for the day and they would spend the whole time in prayer, especially if there was an important need, like a specific amount of money.

Regardless of the subject, there was always a tremendous amount of earnest prayer taking place. As they prayed, they experienced direct answers, and Ivor felt the Lord repeating to him to take notice of different things. Of course he did not realise what was ahead and why the life of prayer was so important. But years later he was grateful for those lessons encouraging him to believe the impossible and trust God had the answer. He also learned about prayer itself, understanding the nature of prayer and its importance in his relationship with his heavenly Father.

Finally the end of his last term came, coinciding with a 10-day conference at the college. Each day speakers addressed the gatherings and in the evenings Ivor was responsible for leading the singing and worship. During the daytime of the last three days he decided to fast and pray in an isolated garden in the college grounds to discover his future beyond his imminent departure. He set himself to spend the time praying, studying the Bible, and reading the writings of well-known Christians like Hudson Taylor, the founder of the China Inland Mission.

The only person to come into the garden was a missionary from South America, who had noticed Ivor's absence from the daytime meetings. On the last day of the conference the man searched out Ivor to find out what he was doing. He listened quietly to Ivor's explanation.

"What are you expecting – signs in the sky, an audible voice?" he asked

"No, but the Lord could do that, if he wanted to," Ivor responded a little defensively.

"You have to be realistic and wise in these things," the missionary said.

"What's unreasonable about fasting and praying and seeking God's will?" Ivor replied.

"There are many missionaries here. Why don't you go speak to them?" the man said.

"That's my problem," Ivor counted. "There are too many of them. So many needs, so many countries . . ."

"That's true," the man agreed, "but listen. Go and place yourself before Norman Grubb of the Heart of Africa Mission," and having said that he left.

Ivor tried to continue his reading but his mind kept returning to the words of the missionary. *He did not tell me to say anything to Norman Grubb, but just to place myself before him,* he thought.

After the evening meal Ivor led the evening worship, followed by several speakers, one of whom was Norman Grubb. At the end of the service Ivor went outside and decided to stand by the doorway. When Norman came out, he would place himself before him.

Streams of people flowed out of the auditorium but Norman was not among them. At last Ivor spotted him, one of the last to come out.

"Wonderful, wonderful, you've come to me," Norman said when he saw Ivor. "I prayed nearly half the night last night for the Lord to send you to me. We've been praying for ten missionaries for the Belgian Congo.[5] We have nine and I believe the Lord wants you to be number ten." Ivor had not said anything to him nor applied for the position.

"Have you any money to pay your fare to the Congo?" Norman asked him.

"No, I don't have any money," Ivor said.

"That doesn't matter," he replied. "We can't talk now but come to my room tomorrow and we'll pray for it."

The next morning Ivor presented himself at Norman's room and he prayed a simple prayer in his customary forthright style.

"Lord, here is a young man come to serve in the Congo. He's number ten. Thank you for providing the tenth, Lord. But Lord, he needs money for equipment and travel. Please provide it. Amen!" Ivor added another short prayer, amazed at the turn of events.

They went out into the corridor towards the main hall, and then Norman remembered he had forgotten his Bible and returned to his room to fetch it. As Ivor continued along the corridor a door opened. A man came out and asked Ivor if he knew where Norman Grubb was. Ivor told him he was coming up behind him and he continued to the main conference room where he sat down to wait for the start of the morning meeting.

A few minutes later Norman appeared in company with the man whom Ivor had met in the corridor. Together they came over to Ivor.

"Don't pray anymore for that money," Norman announced. "We've got it."

The man with Norman had just written out a cheque to cover his expenses. Earlier that morning he had gone to Norman to ask him about Ivor, about whom Norman had spoken the evening before. Every year the man came to the Bible College conference and God usually prompted him to write out a cheque as a donation to the college. The night before, when he was about to write out his cheque, he found he could not sign it. He left it by his bedside until the morning, but again, he had no peace about signing it for the college. When he prayed about it he felt the money was for the young man whom Norman had told him of the evening before.

The man inquired how much Ivor needed and wrote out the cheque. The day before Ivor had no idea where he was destined to work as a missionary. Now he was on his way to the Belgian Congo, and with sufficient money for his needs and his travel.

[1] Act 4, Scene 3.

[2] Ivor's mother lived until she was 92 years old, testifying that the Lord never let her down, providing for her as well as for her missionary sons. When Mary Davies was a girl, before she married, she worked as a household servant for a wealthy Christian family, who led her to the Lord. Years later the family heard that she was widowed and that Ivor was to be a missionary and unable to financially support her. They offered to give her a substantial gift of money so that she could set up a small general store in the front room of her house, and thus earn her living. They wisely advised her never to give credit, thus placing herself in debt. Her grandchildren recalled with great pleasure their Mamgu (Welsh for grandma) and their Aunty Olwen (who spoiled them), selling bottles of milk, large slabs of bacon, big rounds of cheese and delicious sweets in old-fashioned lolly jars.

[3] For more information, see Norman Grubb, *Rees Howells: Intercessor*. After a period of closure the college was purchased, refurbished and reopened by the Singaporean church Cornerstone in 2012.

[4] As well as Ivor and David, Ivor's daughter Miriam also studied at the Bible College of Wales before becoming a WEC missionary.

[5] On independence in 1960 the Belgian Congo became the Democratic Republic of Congo. Between 1971 and 1997 it was renamed Zaire, but is now again known by its name at Independence.

5

An English Rose

Rosalie Deborah was born on 1 October 1903 to Walter and Ada Sore, in a small farming community in Suffolk, England. When Rose was five her mother died. Two months earlier Ada had given birth to Rose's little brother, a difficult birth intensified by a recent incident involving Rose's two-year-old sister Daisy. The little girl had wandered up the lane towards the river, and when her mother in panic chased after her she suffered a brain hemorrhage that led to her death.

Rose's aunty, her mother's sister, took the baby and brought him up with her own. It was a good arrangement, except that the older siblings rarely saw and hardly knew their little brother.

Rose's sister, Lilly, who worked at the farmhouse where their father was employed, came home to look after the motherless family. Lilly was sixteen, the eldest of the seven children. It was a difficult task to take on housekeeping, looking after the four school-aged children and raising Daisy, just a toddler. However, Lil managed well, showing good sense and a committed sense of purpose. Though her cooking was plain she provided plenty of good food, making full use of their father's large vegetable plot with its many fruit trees and currant and gooseberry bushes. In addition, Walter reared pigs and chickens, and the boys kept rabbits.

Rose attended a village school two miles from home and went weekly to Sunday school at the nearby Anglican Church. The family was poor but the children enjoyed a happy childhood with their caring and proficient father. He had an excellent tenor voice, singing in the church choir and entertaining the children with ballads around the fire on a winter's night. Sometimes he told Daisy and Rose stories while the boys read or played games.

After Rose's twelfth birthday, her sister Lil married, and the expectation of managing the household passed to Rose. Her father arranged with the school authorities for her to study for an examination for those who were needed at home for compassionate reasons, allowing her to leave school. Rose was a smart student and an avid reader and had no difficulty passing the exam. Before she was thirteen she had left school and was being shown how to run the household in the tradition of her sister Lil. Her preference, however, was to work in the garden with her father.

In time Walter became friendly with a devout Anglican woman who cooked for a gentleman in the village, and the Sore family grew to know her as she visited the home. Grandma Miriam, as they called her, gave Rose tips on cooking and cleaning, for she was immature and inexperienced. Rose was 21 when their dad married Miriam, the children dropping 'grandma' from her name. Rose searched for employment, and a family friend, Frank Moules, invited her to London for a job interview with an acquaintance who needed a house helper. Rose secured the job and shifted to West Ealing, London.

A year or two before she left for London Rose and her sister Daisy attended some evangelical mission meetings held in the nearby town of Stowmarket, and both of them were born again, accepting Jesus as their Saviour. For the sisters it was an about turn, the beginning of a new life, with Jesus at the centre, for they had been brought up in a church where there was little or no teaching on Jesus as one's personal Saviour.

Their father received their news very well, but Grandma Miriam was not so happy, giving them stern warnings about 'religious mania'.

They found her attitude hard to understand, for she was a God-honouring woman who read her Bible and prayed each morning. But she was influenced by the common idea that one should not talk about one's religion in public.

In London, Rose worked for Miss Hedges and her elderly aunt, and came to regard her employer as "my dear Miss Hedges, my spiritual mother", who amazed with her ability to pray. Rose knew little of the central teachings of Christianity when she arrived from the country, but Miss Hedges taught her the basics of faith and growth in the Lord. Rose lapped it up hungrily, eager to know as much as she could. Each morning they had Bible study and prayer together. Rose called the five years she lived there her private Bible school, for Miss Hedges taught her everything from the rudiments up.

Frank Moules, who had introduced her to Miss Hedges, was the secretary of the Acton Green Railway Mission, under the auspices of the Mission to Railway Men.[1] Rose joined the mission fellowship and the Moules family provided her, and later her sister Daisy, with the hospitality of a second home. The mission hall was located in an underprivileged area, and Rose became involved in leading a class of boys in the Sunday school. It was always a rush to get there in time, after cooking dinner and cleaning up for Miss Hedges, followed by a train trip and a walk to the hall.

One day John Drysdale, Principal of the Emmanuel Bible College, spoke and Rose was very moved by his message. She went forward for prayer, knowing she had many inhibitions and fears. In particular she was afraid of what the Lord would ask of her if she yielded everything to him. In a lengthy discussion with her counsellor she told her she struggled to believe she could be free from her uncertainties and fears, and be effective in God's service.

"Are you willing to be made willing?" the lady asked her.

"Of course, yes," Rose replied.

The lady prayed that the Spirit of God would so come upon her that she would be willing and obedient to His voice and Rose felt God's presence allowing her to yield to him. A new trust filled her heart and she believed the Lord was able to cleanse her of the negative attitudes that hindered her from growing in him. She vowed she would obey him whatever the cost.

The first thing she sensed the Lord asking her to do was to attend a missionary prayer meeting where she was to open her mouth and pray audibly. In her attempt to obey she shook and stammered and burst into tears, a humbling experience. However, she felt victory and the breaking of ties, as joy filled her heart with the witness of the Holy Spirit that he was doing a new work in her life. It was just the beginning, to be followed by more tests of obedience, but she was filled with a new feeling of cleanness and freedom as she allowed the Spirit to take control.

The following eighteen months was a rewarding time of growing in Christian maturity. Then she began to feel uneasy and unsettled, as she came to the conclusion that God wanted her to study at Emmanuel Bible College. As she delayed the decision she grew more miserable. Then one Sunday Frank Moules, preaching at the mission hall, brought a powerful message about Phillip and the Ethiopian eunuch,[2] focusing on the phrase, 'and Phillip ran'.

After he had graphically recounted the story he said that because of Phillip's obedience to the Spirit's prompting, he reached the caravan just at the moment when the eunuch was reading the portion from Isaiah, and Phillip was able to ask him if he understood what he was reading. The preacher challenged his audience.

"The Lord has been dealing with some of you about service for Him," he said, "and you are holding back. If you don't get a move on you are going to miss God's will for your lives. Get moving for God and run, just like Phillip!"

Rose took it as her cue and immediately applied for Emmanuel Bible College.[3] By the beginning of the next college year she had been accepted and was in residence. She greatly enjoyed her two years as a student, with the Lord supplying her financial needs, including her fees. Even her personal needs were often provided in small but miraculous ways.

Once she sensed the call to work in the Belgian Congo Rose realised she should get some nursing experience. So she commenced a rewarding eighteen months midwifery course at Sharoe Green Maternity Hospital[4] in Preston. After gaining her diploma, she knew she needed some general nursing training as well and so applied for a missionary training course at the Bermondsey Medical Mission for Women and Children.[5] Located in South East London, one of the poorest city suburbs, the ten-month training in the clinic, the wards and in the surrounding district equipped her with practical skills, all beneficial for her life in Africa.

When Rose finished her training, she applied to the Heart of Africa Mission to go to the Belgian Congo. She was accepted, transferring to the headquarters in Norwood to quickly prepare for her departure, as the deadline had been set for the provision of ten new missionaries for the Congo. Rose was number nine.

[1] The Railway Mission still operates as a faith-based charity offering pastoral care to the railway community. It was founded in 1881, based in a number of mission halls, and now operates a chaplaincy service.

[2] Acts 8:26-40.

[3] Emmanuel Bible College, near Liverpool, was a 'holiness' Bible college, founded by John Drysdale. Several other family members studied there, as well as Rose and a number of early WEC missionaries. See Norman Grubb's *J D Drysdale, Prophet of Holiness*.

[4] Sharoe Green Hospital opened in 1869, originally owned and managed by Preston Borough Council. By 1980, it had become a substantial 500-bed general hospital; from 1981 many services were moved to the new Royal Preston Hospital, and it closed in 2004.

[5] The charity hospital was established by Dr Selina Fox, operating from 1904 to 1962. See https://ezitis.myzen.co.uk/bermondsey.html

6

The Ten

Few people can claim to be 'living memorials' to another man's work, but that was the case for The Ten – for Ivor, Rose and the eight other missionaries[1] destined for the Belgian Congo in 1932.

Charles Thomas Studd, known as CT Studd, the gifted cricketer and pioneer missionary, died on 16 July 1931 in Ibambi, in the Belgian Congo. It was the year before Ivor Davies' encounter with Norman Grubb during the conference at the Bible College of Wales. It was also the year before Rose Sore and Ivor Davies joined the group headed for the Congo.

CT Studd was one of Britain's most colourful missionaries and the founder of the Heart of Africa Mission (HAM), which in time became WEC International.[2] The period prior to CT's death was a difficult time for the mission organisation. It was troubled by division both overseas and in England over a number of issues, including doctrinal concerns, with its founder and the home committee at odds. A number of missionaries resigned, including half of those working in the Congo who, with others, formed a new missionary association.[3] In addition, the world was hit in 1929 by the Great Depression with its market collapses and unemployment, which seriously limited the flow of funds to missions.

After CT's death Norman Grubb, married to CT's daughter Pauline, became the new home leader of the mission, with the huge task of rebuilding the vision of spreading the gospel across the unevangelised world, as CT Studd had envisioned. One morning as Norman and the mission headquarters team were praying together seeking the Lord, they felt challenged to exercise greater faith in tackling their goal. One of the group said they believed God wanted them to claim ten missionaries to be recruited by the first anniversary of CT Studd's death, as well as the finance to send them.[4]

In the ensuing months they realized their goal. Not only would the ten new missionaries help continue the work CT had established, but they would also be living memorials[5] to him, commemorating his life and contribution. Of the ten, Rose Sore was number nine and Ivor Davies was the final one, applying just ten days before the first anniversary of CT's death.

Though Ivor and Rose never met Studd they soon realised the spirit of the charismatic and provocative Christian leader lived on in the mission organisation he founded. After working as a missionary in China for ten years CT Studd[6] was drawn to Africa in an unusual way. In 1908 in Liverpool a poster advertising a meeting caught his eye – Cannibals Want Missionaries. It prompted him to attend the meeting. CT heard that many had been to Sudan and Central Africa, like explorers, big game hunters, Arabs and traders, European officials and scientists, but no Christians. CT asked himself why no Christians had gone.

Why don't you go he felt God challenge him, and so in 1910 at the age of 50, he set out on an exploratory expedition. Aboard the ship the Lord spoke to him words that were to prove prophetic. The trip was not merely for the Sudan but for the whole unevangelised world. It seemed an impossible task, but the words entered his heart, to become a reality in years to come. CT returned from Africa to Britain convinced God was calling him to establish a work in the Belgian Congo.

Over the next eighteen months, he rallied support for his African venture and laid the foundations for what later became WEC

International. Studd summed up his convictions in one paragraph: "If Jesus Christ be God and died for me, then no sacrifice can be too great for me to make for Him". The words became the motto of the missionary organisation he established.

In 1913 CT and a man less than half his age, Alfred Buxton, departed from Britain for the Congo. The Heart of Africa Mission was in business. Over the next eighteen years, until he died, except for one return visit to Britain in 1915-16, CT lived and worked in the Belgian Congo, establishing a number of viable mission stations with the help of a growing number of missionary co-workers. Priscilla, his wife, worked tirelessly at home to support the endeavour.

CT was a visionary, a pioneer, a founder, and an evangelist, whose strength lay in his amazing zeal and unshakable faith in the Lord, and who left the legacy of a faith enterprise that spread worldwide. The Congolese loved him, calling him Bwana Mukubura, Great White Chief. Within ten years of the beginning of the mission in the jungles of the Congo there were over 50 foreign workers in twelve centres in four Congo provinces. They were involved in medical, educational and vocational training work and in Bible translation. They had appointed elders and evangelists and had begun fledgling churches with an estimated 9,000 converts.[7] It was an amazing record.

Among the early missionaries who came to work under CT and who learnt something of his sacrificial passion were those who would become colleagues of Ivor Davies and Rose Sore. They included Jack Harrison and Jack Scholes, both of whom became future leaders of the Congo work, and veteran Esme Roupell who arrived only three years after CT.

Despite CT's considerable achievements he was a man with idiosyncrasies and faults, like all humans. He often mistook differences of opinion in his colleagues with lack of loyalty and even those close to him found it impossible to differ with him and remain friends.[8] The long-term successful establishment of his missionary vision owed as much to people like his first co-worker Alfred Buxton, his wife Priscilla, and his son-in-law Norman Grubb, as it did to CT himself.

Edith Moules, who arrived in Ibambi four years before CT died, wrote: "I found an old man living in a bamboo house, with a mud floor and a wood fire burning in the middle, a few shelves round the walls with his boxes and some bottles and tins, a rough bed and blankets in the corner, yet burning out for the Lord." She dedicated herself "not to criticise or admire", but to be herself "a living sacrifice"[9] – a wise way of handling such an enigmatic giant of a man of God.

CT's significant contribution to world missionary ventures was certainly worth calling ten new missionaries, including Rose and Ivor, as 'memorials' to mark the first year's anniversary of his death.[10]

[1] The Ten of 1932 were Frank Cripps, Harold Coleman, Elsie Brown, Lily Peckett (who married Frank Cripps), Annie Rose, Vernon Willson, Stephen Cottam, Irene James, Rose Sore (who married Ivor) and Ivor Davies.

[2] WEC initially stood for Worldwide Evangelisation Crusade. In 1982 the letters were changed to stand for Worldwide Evangelisation for Christ.

[3] The Unevangelised Fields Mission, now known as UFM Worldwide.

[4] Janet & Geoff Benge, *Norman Grubb: Mission Builder*, page 127.

[5] Norman Grubb recounts that originally they had in mind, as a more distant goal, a memorial in flesh and blood to C T Studd of 25 new workers. With their struggling situation they realised it was rather an aspiration for the future. After they achieved the ten missionaries they had the courage to pray for an extra 15 to make 25, not just for Africa, but for other areas around the world. Norman Grubb, *After C T Studd*, page 43.

[6] To learn more about CT Studd see Norman Grubb, *C. T. Studd: Cricketer and Pioneer*, and Eileen Vincent, *C T Studd and Priscilla*.

[7] Evan Davies, *Whatever happened to CT Studd's mission?* page 20.

[8] Eileen Vincent, *C T Studd and Priscilla*, page 224.

[9] Norman Grubb, *Mighty Through God: the life of Edith Moules*, pages 16-18. In 1934 Edith née Patton married Percy Moules, another HAM missionary and son of Frank Moules of the Railway Mission; see chapter 4.

[10] By 1936 the target of the sending committee was 75 new missionaries, taking the total number of the people in WEC to 175, more than a 400% increase by the fifth anniversary of CT's death. Evan Davies, *Whatever happened to CT Studd's mission?* page 35.

7

Journey to the Congo

Ivor viewed his surroundings. Curious objects hung on the walls of the Highland Road headquarters of the Heart of Africa Mission in south-east London – tribal drums, spears, and other artifacts endemic to central Africa. The unusual collection, accumulated by homecoming missionaries, seemed strange, even bizarre, to the young Welsh man.

It was 30 July 1932 when Ivor first arrived at the mission headquarters on his way to the Belgian Congo. Three other missionaries were to sail in October with him – Daisy Kingdon, returning to Africa after furlough, having first sailed to the continent in 1925; Irene James, a recruit from Canada and one of The Ten; and Rose Sore, another new recruit with a nursing background.

As was usual for new workers, Ivor came to prepare for his new country and to familiarise himself with the London-based staff. In 1932 that was all the orientation considered necessary, with no formal candidate's course as there was in years to come. Irene James and Daisy Kingdon were already there, while Rose Sore, completing her nurse training, would not arrive much before departure. The mission secretary, Norman Grubb and his wife Pauline also lived and worked at the headquarters.

Ivor found it a busy time. He put his practical skills to work, wall-papering and painting the walls of the centre. There were also medical examinations, vaccinations, and the study of the Kingwana language, a Swahili dialect, widely spoken in those days in the north-east part of the Congo as a trade language.

The hot tropical African climate called for a new wardrobe – sun helmets, shorts, boots, shoes, mosquito boots, socks, Indian gauze vests and pants, woollen belts, and khaki suits that included shorts. Ivor was thrilled with the donation of £120 which meant there was no need to wait for finance to come in or to reduce his gear because of limited funds.

He had time to reflect upon his decision to join the mission. He was delighted with his sense of assurance that he was in the will of the Lord and was pleased he had waited to find the right direction, not listening to other voices which suggested alternative but mistaken options. It was a lesson he determined to remember.

For Ivor's and Rose's close-knit families there was a personal cost to their departure, with its long-term separation and fears for their future safety. A trip to Africa involved many weeks' arduous travel, something one did not undertake on a whim, and it was common knowledge that the continent had claimed a number of missionaries' lives through illness and accident. Rose's father confided to her that he would have liked to accompany her to Africa to see her safely there.

They set sail on the Union-Castle Line's S.S. Llandovery Castle 2, a 10,609 ton steamer, named after a castle ruin in Carmarthenshire, Wales. The ship would carry them 10,700 kilometres through the Mediterranean Sea and Suez Canal to their port of destination, Kilindini, three kilometres from Mombasa, Kenya, followed by the overland journey from the coast to Ibambi in the Belgian Congo, involving a further 2600km. Each missionary had only a steel trunk and a suitcase on board, as their heavier luggage had been sent on ahead. Ivor and Rose farewelled friends and family at the St Pancras railway station and at the Tilbury Docks, happy that they were willing to release them to their chosen calling.

Considering Ivor was heading for a distant foreign continent in the company of three pleasant Christian women one could have forgiven him for thoughts of developing a closer relationship with one of them. However, when Ivor boarded the ship marriage was far from his mind and he did not look around to see if any of them might be his future wife. He had thought Lilian, his girlfriend of six years, would become his wife. But they parted when she went to India. He was determined not to become romantically involved again. On the journey he was polite and helpful, but kept his mind away from matrimonial possibilities.

During the sea trip of 23 days Ivor shared his cabin with three young men his own age whom he found more worldly than himself but nevertheless very pleasant. One night one of them entered the cabin when Ivor was on his knees praying. The young man tip-toed in as quietly as he could and undressed. When Ivor got into bed and read his Bible the young man stood in doubt for a minute and then knelt down and said his prayers. Next morning, when Ivor returned from the bathroom, his three cabin mates, deep in conversation, suddenly went quiet, obviously in discussion about him. Ivor knew they were watching him and he hoped his witness was honouring to the Lord.

Later, as Ivor returned to the cabin, he found the praying young man reading one of his own books by C. T. Studd. Ivor found his language coarse at times but he was sure he might have had a good influence on him, if it were not for the negative impact of his companions.

The missionaries scheduled themselves busy days, usually beginning at 9.00am with an hour of prayer, followed by another hour of Kingwana language exercises and an hour and a half of study and letter writing. In the afternoon there was more language study, which included reading the Kingwana New Testament, and more prayer, with free time after dinner. On Sunday evenings one of them played the piano in the lounge while the rest sang hymns, unfazed by the stares of other passengers, some of whom, Ivor surmised, threw their Christianity overboard when they cruised out of the Thames.

On its way through the Mediterranean the ship called in at Genoa in Italy and sailed near the island of Stromboli off the coast of Sicily where the volcano erupted with a spectacular display of flames. Once in Egypt they donned their sun helmets and perspired in the heat, spotting with fascination new sights through the Suez Canal, such as their first camel train. During a stopover in Sudan Ivor was impressed with the first Africans he saw, singing at their work even though they carried terribly heavy burdens. He saw a man carrying on his back half a dozen car tyres in a wooden case, his legs bowing under him as he struggled to manage his load.

Ivor was appalled at the behaviour of some of his fellow Englishmen, whom he felt treated the Africans worse than dogs. He wrote to his family, "I saw one white man walk into a crowd of them, instead of going around, only to make them part for him – the hypocrite. And these are the kind who say the missionary is a nuisance."

They arrived in Kenya after three weeks aboard the ship, landing in the morning at Kilindini and departing by train for Nairobi from the docks in the early evening, winding and turning all the way from Mombasa up to Nairobi for twenty hours. Ivor was delighted to travel through 320 kilometres of game reserve, where he caught sight of wild animals such as antelopes and zebra, and interesting vegetation: trees carrying new leaves, old leaves, blossoms and fruit, all on the same tree.

Overland journeys across the African heartland had long been difficult. The famous Welsh-American journalist and explorer, Sir Henry Stanley, overcame many obstacles while trekking the Congo before he found his man and uttered the memorable words, "Dr. Livingstone, I presume?" Though travel was easier by 1932, when a lesser-known Welsh man and his three female companions journeyed from Nairobi to Ibambi, in the north-east corner of the Congo, the journey was still arduous and complicated.

From Nairobi they travelled by train to the Ugandan town of Namasagali on the Victoria Nile, where they caught a boat for Masindi across Lake Kyogo, spending the night on board. It was there they experienced their first of many impressive African thunderstorms, which in time they grew used to.

A car-lorry met them at Masindi Port, also on the banks of the Victoria Nile, and they drove 110 kilometres to Butiaba, on the shores of Lake Albert, where they boarded the steam ship Robert Coryndon,[1] to cross the lake. At the mouth of the Nile they embarked on another ship, the Lugard, sleeping on her until next morning when they sailed up the White Nile. Ivor and his companions marvelled at many strange and beautiful sights along the river and in the forest, before they arrived at Rhino Camp, merely a tin shed.

The lengthy journey continued. Harold Williams, an Australian missionary working with the mission, met them in the mission truck and, after a break, drove them two hours to Arua, still in Uganda, where their heavy luggage was waiting. They stayed the night with Mr Voller, a missionary working for Africa Inland Mission. Early next morning they crossed the border into the Congo and passed through customs, a tedious process of four and a half hours, before they were on the road again by mid-morning, bound for Ibambi, the mission headquarters.

Ivor found it a fascinating drive, seeing wild animals crossing the road right in front of the vehicle. They rode through the night, right into the heart of the forest, stopping only for meals. About 6.30 in the morning they reached Wamba, the station where Harold worked and after a meal and a wash, set off mid-morning for Ibambi, the final two-hour stretch of the gruelling journey. In spite of his tiredness Ivor was struck with the beauty of the landscape in the daylight, the bright green vegetation of the forest growing right up to the narrow strip of red-brown earth that formed the road. Everywhere there were villages of mud and bamboo huts scattered among groves of banana trees.[2]

Nothing could have prepared the new missionaries for the rapturous reception awaiting them. Thousands had heard of their arrival and came to welcome them, stretching out their hands to clasp and greet the new missionaries and receive them with song and dance.

The Ibambi Station, home to two hundred Africans and several European missionaries, was situated in the Ituri Province, one of the most heavily populated areas in the Congo. Ivor was impressed with the attractive appearance of the station. A wide road exposing terra-cotta red earth ran through its centre, lined with palms planted by the missionaries. On either side, set well back from the road, were bamboo houses for the European workers, as well as a large bamboo storehouse and church. Behind them, among more palm trees, were African huts housing the Congolese living on the station. A mere twelve years previously, virgin forest covered the entire site. The centre included its own small medical clinic and separate schools for the local boys and girls.

The mission station, CT's headquarters in his final four years, was to be Ivor's work base for the next three years.

[1] The Robert Coryndon sailed with passengers and cargo between various Ugandan and Congolese ports on Lake Albert between 1930 and 1965, when it was abandoned in the former port of Butiaba, where she lies today.

[2] Janet & Geoff Benge, *Norman Grubb: Mission Builder*, page 171; description taken from Norman Grubb's notes.

8

Missionary Novice

Ivor felt a complete failure. Was his missionary career over before it had hardly begun? The experience of seeing African life up close caused Ivor to long for an escape from the realities of mission life. A revealing glimpse of the actualities of Congolese life was a devastating shock to his British sensibilities.

One evening a missionary nurse invited Ivor to accompany her on her rounds to the nearby villages. Ivor eagerly seized the opportunity, as he had not yet been inside any village huts. As she treated the patient by the fire he followed her, bending low to go through the doorway, the sole opening. When he straightened up, his eyes smarted sharply with the pall of smoke filling the upper atmosphere of the hut. Then a nauseating smell assailed his nose. He quickly bobbed down low to clear his eyes, and realised the sickening odour came from the appalling tropical sore the nurse had come to treat. He stood stock-still in shock, trying to control the surge of queasiness that welled up within, while the nurse patiently cleaned the abscess, before continuing from hut to hut, treating other ailments.

It was not only the infections that distressed Ivor as he struggled to stop retching. It was also the squalor. Small mounds of faeces dotted the yard. The people had no toilets inside their huts and instead used the area outside. As he and the nurse moved about in the darkness they had to be careful not to step on any of the deposits. In hut after hut Ivor saw further examples of poor hygiene and disease which shocked him to the core.

"Lord, I can't love these people," he cried silently as they returned to the station. "I thought I loved them, but the lack of hygiene and the filth is too much."

In the following days he felt deep condemnation because of his failure to cope. *Perhaps he would have to go home if he couldn't come to terms with village life.*

"Lord, you helped me back in Wales," he cried out in desperation. "You changed my mother's attitude and you put me through Bible college. You led me to come out here. You must have an answer for the way I feel."

God spoke to his heart, assuring him he did have the answer, and Ivor began to see the people through the eyes of the Lord. He had failed because he tried to love the people with his own inadequate love. He had to love them with the love of God, understanding that Jesus died on the cross for them just as much as he died for himself.

Understanding did not come in a flash. He had to work at it. But as his empathy for the people grew, relief flooded his spirit and he wondered how he could have considered leaving the Congo.

The field leader gave every new missionary a Kingwana name to enable the indigenous people to address them in a pronounceable style. Sometimes the names were simply derived from their European names, such as the Harrisons' titles of Harri and Ma Harri. Rose Sore became Ma Mupanda, Mupanda being the Kingwana term for Sower which sounded similar to Sore. Mary Rees became known as Ma Risasi, as risasi meant 'bullets' or 'gunpowder' which resembled her European name in sound and her character in spirit.

Ivor's African name was Kumi which simply meant Ten, his number in the memorial Ten. Sometimes the Congolese coined what they felt were more appropriate names and rarely were these names flattering. In Ivor's case the Congolese preferred a name which meant 'the man without a stomach', for Ivor was very skinny as a young man before he was married.

The diet of the Ibambi Europeans produced mixed reactions. Ivor knew the mouths of his Welsh family would water if they could see him eating the local pineapples, bananas and pawpaws. The fruit was indeed delicious, but when they ate the same items at every meal they longed for a change. However there was no money at the time to buy fowls. Ivor's mother sent him a tin of tongue, providing enough for dinner and the next morning, a welcome variation to the monotonous regime.

Sometimes food shipped out by his family did not improve in transportation. His mother sent a cake which arrived looking rather green and included some small stowaways that had crept into the cake container. Rose's excellent cooking skills saved the day when she salvaged the best parts of the cake and turned it into a very edible pudding, enjoyed by all the station missionaries.

The locals were more imaginative in their choice of food sources. For example, they killed a large snake, about four metres long and 100 millimetres thick, which they cut up, cooked and ate.

Ivor had his own room in a rectangular three-bedroom bamboo structure with a grass thatch roof, built to accommodate the single male missionaries. Other buildings on the station employed a daub-and-wattle method of wall construction, using the local red clay and bamboo. Within Ivor's room were the bare necessities: a bamboo-slat bed, a bedside table, a bookshelf and a few containers with good seals.

Ivor reached the ominous conclusion he was not the only one in residence in his room. He quickly learned not to leave his boots on the floor or anything else likely to be nibbled by rodents and it became second nature to put all food in screw-top containers for safety.

Lizards lived in the bamboo walls but were an asset in killing the noisy crickets and the abundant cockroaches which came out in the evenings, along with the rats. White ants were plentiful, travelling inside their small mud tunnels and doing much damage to the house structure over time. However, they were beneficial, for they cleared up all rubbish so nothing was left to rot and smell. Snakes were another problem. Ivan found a discarded snake skin in his room, so he knew one had visited him. But he discovered flies and other flying insects were not as bad as he had imagined, much the same as in England in the heat of summer.

The Ibambi station had the luxury of a well, unlike other stations where water was drawn from rivers or streams and boiled before use. Ivor's lad carried washing water in buckets for him from the well. If he wanted a bath, his boy warmed the water and Ivor stood up to his ankles in the canvas camp bath, about two feet square in size, and washed himself down with a sponge he had purchased in Port Said. If he was very careful he could just sit down in it.

Ivor imagined he would begin straightaway preaching to crowds of locals, but his notion was shattered when he found himself directed into the building trade. When he grumbled inwardly that he did not come out to Africa to build houses the Lord reminded him that he vowed to undertake any task. There was, in fact, a pressing need for more buildings, something that would continue into the future.

The station's twenty bamboo structures were constantly damaged by tropical storms and had to be rebuilt every three or four years. CT Studd did not bother to construct in brick at any of the stations. He was an evangelist with his primary focus on spreading the gospel. Consequently bamboo, timber and grass were his obvious choices of construction materials. Buildings could be quickly erected, the materials were readily available, and more importantly, they were the ones with which the African workmen were familiar. If the mission stations were moved to better locations, or if the missionaries were forced to leave the country, building in brick would have been a waste of time.

By 1932, when Ivor arrived, the Heart of Africa Mission had established a total of twelve stations in a 31,000 square kilometre area. The mission had come a long way from its humble beginnings in 1913 with two lone missionaries, CT Studd and Alfred Buxton. Under CT's leadership, until his death in 1931, more than 120 missionaries worked with the mission, bringing radical changes to many lives. Thousands became Christians, turning from paganism, and many benefitted from the simple medical treatment supplied by the missionaries. In addition, hundreds of children learned to read and write.

Ivor and his three women companions arrived as Jack Harrison,[1] CT's right-hand man and successor, was beginning to take the mission work into a new phase. Though from a humble background and limited schooling Jack Harrison was a multi-gifted man, who had worked very closely with Studd for nine years through the last stressful days of the old man's journey.[2] With discipline and humility he played a powerful role in maintaining unity, trust and stability among the European workers and the African church, leading the mission into a time of necessary consolidation. His colleagues paid him a great compliment when they said he had the exceptional ability to 'think black'.[3]

Under Studd the work had expanded quickly, but Harri wanted to ensure that the existing work was consolidated before any further major expansion took place. He felt it imperative that the converts be better trained so they could be more effective as pastors and preachers. He knew that a strong indigenous church, one of their major aims, would never succeed without properly trained local leaders.

When Harri became field leader he also decided to build in brick because he believed Ibambi's location would be permanent. Time proved him to be correct. He saw that much effort was wasted by having to regularly rebuild the bamboo buildings. So Ivor was given the task of overseeing the making of bricks and training African workmen to lay them. The fact that Ivor's father and two brothers-in-law were masons, and that he had been a house decorator, made him the closest thing to an expert brick-maker among the missionaries. The reality was that he had no better understanding of the brick-making process than anyone else.

Ivor set to his task by sending six men to points around the property to dig down an arm's length and return with a jam jar filled with the soil extracted from the bottom of the hole. He poured water in each jar and allowed the sediment to settle before examining them to determine how much sand, clay and soil was in each sample. From the samples he chose the site which he thought would produce the best clay to make bricks.

He began making them two at a time with a little machine he managed to obtain, and he taught the local men how to do it. They produced 20,000 bricks which they laid in long drying sheds. Ivor then consulted an encyclopedia to discover how to kiln-bake the bricks, learning there was an art to ensuring the bricks were stacked to allow the steam to escape from the kiln. They assembled the bricks into a pyramid shape but did not have quite enough to finish it at the top. So Ivor decided to use bricks that were not completely dry for the last three or four layers.

They finished the kiln and Ivor left two men in charge of stoking the fire throughout the night. He returned to his room for a time of Bible study and prayer, when he came on a surprising verse in Isaiah 9:10 which he had not noticed before. Just as he read the words, 'the bricks are fallen down,' he heard the pitter-patter of African feet outside and someone pounding on his door.

"Bwana! Bwana Kumi!" a voice cried. "Come quickly. The bricks have fallen down and my friend is underneath them!"

They rushed back to the kiln and frantically freed the man buried under the bricks. Fortunately he was not burnt but virtually all the bricks were broken. Ivor was very discouraged, wondering what the Congolese thought of his mistake. After the kiln was fired the heat and steam intensified but could not escape because of the half-dry bricks on top, and in time the whole pile burst and collapsed.

The next attempt at brick kiln-firing was a success and by March 1933 work started on the first brick structures – a storehouse and an office. Ivor's next task was to teach his six helpers how to construct in brick. It was not easy. After they dug a trench Ivor had them place a string line along it between pegs at each end. Then he demonstrated how to lay the bricks, instructing them to watch him as he did it. But as they laid the bricks they pushed up against the string and soon the wall was no longer even.

Ivor pointed out their bricks were not straight and he instructed them not to push against the line but just to work up to it. He went away to another job and when he came back he saw they still had problems. They could see the string line was not close enough to the bricks, so they used a bent leaf stem to hook around the string and attached the other end of the leaf to the bricks, bringing the string back in toward the bricks they had laid.

Then Ivor had another issue. His workers watched him close one eye to see if the bricks were in a straight line and they misunderstood what he was doing. They thought the answer to achieving a straight line was in the closing of an eye; so they attempted to work with one hand over one eye! It took effort and patience, but in time Ivor's workers became expert builders.

At the same time, Ivor appreciated that he could teach them more than practical skills, using examples of life on the station to communicate principles of biblical living. So while he taught the importance of straight lines for building he also talked about the straightness of their hearts and their relationship to the Lord. By working among them and by his own example he shared spiritual truths which were, at that stage, more effective than instruction in a formal Bible school setting. In time, the men became both practical workers and devout pastors.

One weekend Ivor made his first attempt at preaching the gospel, but it was not easy. While his command of Kingwana had rapidly improved he had problems conveying his message. He and Harri travelled 21 kilometres by car to a village, where they took two services in an old barn-shaped bamboo house. The congregation comprised 25 Congolese, each with just a loin cloth around their middle. Harri and Ivor both spoke in Kingwana. Ivor read a passage about the Lord walking on the sea and spoke about it. He later wrote home to his family, "Well, I suppose it was good for the first attempt, but I nearly failed to bring Peter out of the water. I struggled through and out he came."

While Ivor concentrated on the building work at Ibambi Rose exercised her nursing skills in the dispensary. The medical complaints were very different from those she encountered during her training in England. One major problem was the limited range of drugs at their disposal with which to treat the nasty infections frequently met. The treatment offered at the Ibambi and the eleven other dispensaries was in great demand, with long queues of patients standing outside.

Rose's duties included assembling supply packages to be dispatched from the main station, Ibambi, out to the other stations. As her command of Kingwana improved she helped in the Ibambi girls' school and trekked to the villages to undertake medical work and to share the gospel.

At Christmas most of the Ibambi missionaries spread out around the area. The Harrisons went to Deti for the opening of a new church built by volunteer local Christians. Rose and Herman Meyers went to outstations on their own, while Stephen Cottam, another member of The Ten, remained at Ibambi. Ivor spent his first Christmas, two months after his arrival, at an outstation, two and a half hours' walk from Ibambi, and many kilometres away from any other European.

When the locals heard that the white man had arrived they gathered around Ivor's house, conversing with each other loudly and cheerfully. To the sound of their merriment Ivor ate his Christmas dinner alone – chicken soup, manioc root with a small knob of butter, two bananas with a cup of condensed milk, and water. And yet he was very contented, writing home that it was the best Christmas he had spent.

It was a great joy next morning to tell the story of Jesus's birth and death and to explain their meaning. Other meetings followed in the afternoon and in the evening by the light of a lantern. Ivor was impressed by the fine Christians there, like the Congolese evangelist who knew the scriptures as well as Ivor did, and the high standard of Christian faith, due in part to the previous work of CT Studd.

[1] For Jack Harrison's life story, see Norman Grubb, *Successor to C.T. Studd.*

[2] Evan Davies, *Whatever happened to CT Studd's mission?* page 42.

[3] Norman Grubb, *Successor to C. T. Studd,* page 130.

9

A Sinister Reality

To the casual observer the Belgian Congo may have seemed a paradise of abundance, for the country had many admirable assets: mysterious and unusual animals, a colourful endemic plant life, rich mineral deposits and the potential to grow virtually any crop.

However, a closer look at the area in the 1930s revealed a sinister underside. Fear, above all else, dictated Congolese life, with love virtually unknown. Witchcraft, pagan rituals and beliefs, and forms of slavery – dating back many centuries – worked together to inflict misery and injustice on the indigenous population. Cannibalism, though outlawed by the government, was still practised in remote areas.

On top of the culture of pagan wretchedness was the troubled history of colonialism. In 1885 King Leopold II of Belgium established the Congo Free State as his personal privately-owned domain, violently exploiting the natural resources, especially of rubber and ivory, and perpetrating dreadful atrocities through his administrators and traders. Responding to public protests the government of Belgium took over the territory in 1908, ending forced labour. They built schools and roads, but did little to include Congolese in the administration of the country.

Into this tragic arena the missionaries brought their message of hope and release from the bondage of fear and evil.

According to animist Congolese, and the witch doctors who reinforced the view, no one died of natural causes. The witch doctors claimed to know why an individual died, the usual explanation being that a curse had been placed on the deceased. The animists worshipped particular trees and, out of the wood, made idols which the witch doctors used to connect with the spirit world. Those forces were powerful and evil. The witch doctors described what they looked like, causing much fear among the people.

Love was hardly known, and if the word 'love' was expressed it was regarded as a sign of weakness. Talk of the love of God by the missionaries came as a great surprise to the Congolese. The witch doctors objected to the Christian message. They opposed Africans living on the mission stations by planting items around the compound in shallow holes, such as bark or an animal bone, using them to formulate their curses.

Sometimes people became paralysed or sick as a result, and the missionaries responded by holding prayer meetings to pray specifically for the affected person. Resulting healings demonstrated that God himself was stronger than any power the witch doctors could manifest. Gradually the people realized the truth of what the missionaries were saying and they came to see that God's strength and power was more powerful than witchcraft.

Some of the local practices were brutal and cruel. Young boys were initiated into their tribes and clans by circumcision and other rites at the age of sixteen to eighteen, though sometimes they were younger. The initiation rites included ceremonies which were harsh and unhealthy, like forcing boys to walk through a large pit which the village had used as a toilet.

Beatings as part of the initiation were common. Boys were taken out into the forest and beaten across the legs until their calves became twice the normal size. They were blind-folded and had marks cut into their bodies, with juices rubbed in so that, as the wounds healed, raised ridges or shapes resulted.

The indigenous Christians wanted alternatives so they could avoid the pagan initiations. Accordingly the missionaries arranged for trained local medics to undertake circumcisions, thus avoiding the unhygienic conditions of the witchdoctors, which often caused temporary or permanent damage to the boys' health. The missionaries also organised Congolese teachers to teach the boys about their culture, things essential for them to learn as Africans. The temptation was always present to retreat to pre-Christian practices, especially at times like a marriage or a funeral, which formerly involved practices of the witchdoctor. The inducement was even greater for an important family.

'Human leopards' stalked people at night, providing another source of terror. They were men who fastened short iron claws to their hands to rip open their victims' faces and necks. In 1933 Ivor, aware of the powerful darkness in people's lives, wrote that 36 people had been known to have been killed by 'leopards' between Ibambi and Wamba since he had arrived. It was a matter of speculation how many others were killed in the forest without the whites knowing about them. What was done with the bodies, they were unable to guess, except the horrible possibility of cannibalism, which was officially forbidden.

Although cannibalism was less evident in the 1930s than when the Heart of Africa Mission workers first arrived in 1913 it was still practised in the more remote areas. One clan, by agreement, would hand over its dead for consumption by another clan, despite government laws to the contrary. As soon as government officials heard of an instance of cannibalism they acted immediately to stop it. Despite the Congo's long history of violence and cannibalism the missionaries themselves rarely felt in personal danger from the indigenous population.

Some of the things they heard and witnessed, however, were unnerving. In a village near Ibambi the residents showed Ivor a medium-sized drum covered with a skin.

"That's the skin of a white man," they told him. In another village the residents gave him a present saying it was goat's meat. In the morning Ivor's assistants told him a recent feast had involved the eating of a dead man. The villagers had passed over most of the body to another clan but had 'graciously' gifted the remainder to Ivor! One Congolese convert related to the missionaries how, as a child, he had watched his struggling mother being hacked to pieces, to be eaten. Outlawing cannibalism could only achieve so much. Ultimately the answer came through changing people's hearts.

Occasionally the Congolese suffered severe injustices at the hands of people who abused the power of their position. In some instances a corrupt government official took advantage of those he governed or a trader cheated the farmers out of a fair price for their produce. However, the majority of abuse and cruelty was inflicted by a few of the Congolese chiefs, who had more direct and dictatorial control of the people living in their tribal areas.

Ivor wrote: "People say there are no slaves today; well, I beg to differ. I often see slaves out here. There are things going on here today nearly, if not as bad as, the times of the rubber atrocities." He saw the regime as similar to feudalism in England under the lords and barons. The Belgians owned the whole lot, chiefs and all. If the Belgians wanted a road made or cotton planted they talked to the chiefs. The chiefs owned the village land, the people and other material things. The chief told the head man who told the village heads who ordered the people. If the people refused they were flogged, hit, kicked, fined or imprisoned; and if they did not accede they were sent to the mines or deported.

If the chief saw a good-looking girl he wished to add to his wives he sent a man for her, and her family dared not refuse. If the chief wanted chickens or goats he sent his soldiers to fetch them without making any payment. He regarded all as his own and if they refused they were beaten and the items taken from them. The soldiers were not free, but had to do as the chief ordered. If a soldier became a

Christian and could not obey the chief's underhand demands his life was in jeopardy. Becoming a Christian could cost a person their life.

The local people never questioned heaven or hell or the power of Satan, knowing the reality only too well. Belgian traders, tyrannical chiefs, medicine men, witch doctors and their own lives were proof of the work of Satan. On the other hand they knew without being asked that the missionaries were the servants of the Most High God.

Some of them became very fine Christians. Accepting the message of life in Christ was at times costly. For example, seven Christians were put in prison for not working on Sunday. One of them, an old man, was asked by the chief if he had anything to say, and he replied:

"Chief, I am only an old man, a nobody; I am like one of the animals in the sight of man, and maybe no good for work. But there is one thing I do know, and that is, I am completely dedicated to Christ." One of the chief's soldiers then knocked him over and he was put in prison.

Many of the Congolese readily accepted the concept of spending eternity with God after death. Previously they believed their soul would pass into an animal. It was when Christianity challenged deep-rooted customs that there could be great resistance. Polygamy, for instance, was one of the most contentious issues confronting the churches in developing African countries.

In the Belgian Congo of the 1930s polygamy had a tremendous effect on society. Baby girls were often sold to middle-aged chiefs as wives, for the number of wives reflected a chief's wealth and his standing in society. Some chiefs had more than 100 wives, most no better than slaves. When a chief died his wives automatically became the property of the chief's heir. The situation also denied single men the chance to find a woman to marry.

One young girl called Fulani was used by her brother as payment for the chief's daughter, whom the brother wanted to marry. Though

Fulani was but a child, she became one of the chief's many wives, the slave of them all. She hated her ugly, dirty and frequently drunk husband, running back to her nearby former home. She was soon discovered and dragged back to the chief, who tied her hands, suspended her by the rafters of his hut, whipped her, and then left her hanging for two nights. As a result one hand came off at the wrist and the other, though intact, was rendered useless.

The chief later died. Fulani happily married again, had a child, was converted to Christianity, and came to live on the Nala Mission Station. Though destined to live her life disabled because of the chief's cruelty her passion became telling people about the Lord.

The missionaries fought numerous battles to protect girls from fathers desiring to sell their daughters to chiefs or other men for little more than a few bars of iron. In Congolese custom fathers had a right to marry their daughters to whoever they chose.

Harri became embroiled in a stressful situation involving a young girl who attended the mission school. Her father, who claimed he was a Christian, wanted to sell her to the chief who already had dozens of wives. The girl, however, wished to remain in school. If she married him she would go and live with the other wives, enduring a life of misery and pain, purely because her father wanted to please the chief and to receive a payment.

Harri told the father he would not give the girl over until there was a local gathering of indigenous Christians, where he would hand the girl to her father in front of everyone, telling them the full story. Unfortunately the law was on the side of the father. Ivor and the other missionaries experienced deep distress over the way the children were treated, feeling helpless to find a solution.

Because the girls received little love from their husbands they were frequently unfaithful. Some found a younger man closer to their own age and attempted to flee with them. Others submitted to the demands of another man simply because he asked them. Some chiefs punished unfaithfulness by holding their wives in guarded compounds or by cattle-branding their wives' arms with the chief's name. Ivor observed that women who were treated all their lives as a commodity for a man's pleasure came to believe that was their duty.

Congolese homes dealt out harsh discipline to the children. Sometimes if a child was disobedient the father or mother would tie his legs with rope and fasten it to the roof of the hut so the child hung upside down. The parent then hit their bare skin as if the child was a bit of leather. Children consequently learned at a young age to lie, their proficiency a real challenge. They were a marked contrast to the 30 or 40 children living with their parents on the mission station and under Rose Sore's charge. To hear them singing hymns as they played was a real pleasure. They received names like Furaha, meaning joy, or Kupenda, meaning love, and Paulo or Timoti.

Ivor disagreed with people who said the Africans did not understand sin and right from wrong before the missionaries arrived. They knew, and would say so. Before the missionaries arrived the Africans meted out death as the penalty for adultery. They also had a keen sense of fair judgment. It did not matter to them if a case was settled against them, as long as they saw it was a fair judgment. They would say "Iko muzuri" – it is good.

At the mere sight of missionaries some locals took flight and hid in the forest. Later when asked why they fled, they might say they knew they were sinners but did not want to believe that day; another day would do. Some accepted aspects of Christianity but not everything. Others accepted Christ but soon fell away from their faith. It was hard for them to stand because of the strong influence of their relatives and their very real fear of evil spirits.

But many continued loyal to Christ, with a deep-rooted faith and a willingness to risk all for their belief. Ivor described one such man, Zebo, whom he compared to Paul. The skin on his back was much thicker than was natural due, Ivor believed, to the numerous floggings he had received from his chief for refusing to break the Lord's commandments.

In another village the chief was a strong Christian, but years ago had been a soldier, killing people and even helping the Belgians to cut off hands during the Rubber Atrocities. But he became a delightful old man, as gentle as a lamb.

"Bwana," he told Ivor, "I have much to thank the Lord Jesus for. I was a terrible sinner and nothing was too vile for me to do. But when I accepted Jesus he washed my blood-stained heart with his own holy blood and now, oh, what a change. My heart is one of love, not sin. Jesus is wonderful." Ivor concluded it was worth all his discomfort to bring the gospel to people like the village head, who put many western Christians in the shade.

The missionaries heard new converts begging for Bible teachers to visit their home villages. But there were insufficient missionaries to adequately cover the whole region, with some areas visited infrequently or not at all. Yet some very fine churches were established by the Congolese, following the briefest of visits by a missionary.

The dearth of teachers highlighted the need to train more indigenous Bible teachers. Ivor and Rose arrived in the Congo just as plans were being made for the mission's first Bible school at Ibambi. The plans were part of Harri's strategy of consolidation and Ivor would play an important role in the construction of the school.

10

Station Conferences

In July 1932 more than 7000 people met together in harmonious fellowship. Skeptical onlookers had warned that a huge gathering of local people would only bring trouble. Traders, officials and cotton agents all watched, anticipating disaster if Congolese Christians from numerous tribes came together for the week-long conference. However, the missionaries continued to plan ahead, praying for a successful event to mark the first anniversary of CT Studd's death, seeking and gaining government permission.

From all over the Heart of Africa Mission[1] region the different tribes and clans gathered, some of them previously vicious enemies. Many travelled hundreds of kilometres on foot, singing as they filed into the Ibambi compound, filling to overflowing the hastily constructed open-sided accommodation huts. The attendance exceeded all expectations, for some wondered if the commitment of the Congolese would wane following the death of the highly charismatic and loved CT.

There was no shortage of food. Chiefs brought in lorry loads of provisions, the missionaries alone given 1500 eggs and 450 chickens. The honesty and generosity confounded local traders and government officials who alleged, sometimes through bitter experience, that the Congolese were "liars and cheats". Former enemy chiefs, who had once placed curses upon each other, stood together drinking tea and sharing spoons. All lost property was handed in, to be returned to its owners. The meetings went on for hours and continued with singing and prayers around fires throughout the night.

Arriving a few months later Ivor and Rose heard of the success of the conference and appreciated the decision to plan for two conferences in 1933. The first in mid-year was to be a missionary conference, followed around Christmas by one for the Congolese Christians. As a result, the station programme became busier, in addition to the usual activity in the schools and medical centre.

Ivor's task was to oversee the construction work. The first planned brick buildings, the storeroom and office, were to double as accommodation for the thirty HAM missionaries attending. Ivor supervised three groups of men: one building in brick; another constructing in wood; and a third of 30 untrained new labourers preparing poles for a new school.

Harri and Ma Harri were frequently away from Ibambi and Ivor, the raw recruit, felt unprepared for the challenges of management on the station. He found little time to write home and answer the growing pile of letters, which his lad reminded him needed answering. There were many other matters to attend to on the station with its live-in population of 200 to 250. People wanted his advice. Should they go and visit a sick relative? Would Ivor advise them about the payment of a debt they owed? Would he counsel someone about their sin and need to renew their relationship with God? Would he intervene in a dispute where someone had spoken critically of another? Despite his long list of duties Ivor still found time to teach at the Ibambi boys' school. He suffered his first bout of serious malaria in mid-1933, though it seemed to do little to dampen his spirit.[2]

Other issues increased the busyness. Ibambi was frequented by missionaries from other stations and missions, and by traders – Greek, Russian, French, Arab, and German – requiring help. Some needed assistance with cars that had mechanical faults, or with the loan of a vehicle. Others wanted medical aid, a typewriter fixed or a printing order on Ibambi's printing press, ably run by Frank Cripps, who was also one of The Ten.

In March 1933 Harri announced his decision to replace the old Ibambi bamboo church building with a new auditorium. But there were not enough workmen on the station to cope with the large quantity of building work. He called the evangelists together and told them his idea: he wanted them to encourage the local Christians to give one day a week to the Lord to build the new church.

After he shared his plan everyone – Congolese and missionaries – went out to the villages, and announced the proposal. Later they returned for the 4.30 pm service, and each evangelist reported their peoples' responses. At that point the need for a replacement was underscored in a most dramatic manner. During the meeting a tremendous storm rolled in, the likes of which most of them had not experienced before. Dense torrential rain, impossible to see through, teemed down and violent winds tore through the building, rattling the bamboo and beating the fronds on the roof.

The Congolese scrambled up, ready to run outside, but the Harris, Rose, Stephen Cottam and Ivor, not wanting to cause panic, kept their seats. The people stood and began to sing a chorus. Then, above the roar of the wind there came the shattering sound of poles cracking and thatching tearing from the roof. Everyone made a dive for the doors and windows and the whole great building collapsed and crumpled down on top of their heads. Ivor crawled back under the wreckage in search of lost victims, but found none. In all the chaos of debris no one was hurt.

Plans were drawn-up for a brick church to hold 1000 people, but the project was put aside until after the July missionary conference, so the other buildings required for the first event could be completed on time. By June, three months into the brick work, the storeroom-cum-accommodation was ready for the roof. It measured fifteen by four and a half metres and almost seven metres high.

That same month four new missionary recruits arrived at Ibambi, one of whom was Eric Smith, a joiner by trade. He and Ivor worked as a team, Eric's expertise taking the building programme into top gear. They later became related by marriage when Eric married Daisy Sore, Rose's sister, after she arrived there in 1935. With all his outdoor work Ivor's lean legs, arms and face had become bronzed by the sun, posing a stark contrast to the pale and plump complexions of the new recruits. As the missionary conference fast approached Ivor, his team of bricklayers, and Eric put the finishing touches to the accommodation block. Ivor was extremely pleased with the end result – straight walls and perfect arches over the windows and doors.

On Sundays Ivor trekked to one of the surrounding villages to preach the gospel. The little children ran away from him, yelling at the top of their voices, shouting "Musungu" – white man. If the parents brought them to shake his hands, they were at first stiff with fright until he won them over. Sometimes the people were very receptive, downing their tools in their cotton fields to listen to what the Musungu had to say.

He became fluent in Kingwana. Being bilingual in Welsh and English assisted his efforts to learn the African language. He discovered that Welsh and Kingwana were similar in rhythm, and if he started to pray in Welsh he could not help slipping in and out of Kingwana.[3]

One Sunday he had a wonderful experience. Harri asked him to go to a village where a man wanted to burn his witchcraft tools. He took with him Fred Dunbar, one of the new missionaries, as well as a Congolese teacher who had previous dealings with the man. When they arrived he asked for the drum to be beaten, and spoke to them, leading in singing and prayers.

He then gave them time to discuss the gospel among themselves. More people came and the meeting continued for three hours. Three men and two women indicated that they wished to believe in the Lord and the burning of the witchcraft instruments followed. Ivor was deeply touched to see the man standing watching his items burning and singing hallelujah. He was filled again with a real sense of the significance of what he was doing.

In addition, Ivor began to see spiritual results among his workers at Ibambi. Thirteen of his workmen, including four of his bricklayers, offered to go as evangelists to preach the gospel to tribes who had not received the gospel. It encouraged him to train others so that they too might become teachers.

Prayer was all-important, given the forces of evil in the environment in which the missionaries worked. They prayed for more Congolese to become Christians and for deliverance from the difficult situations they encountered. They also regularly prayed for new concessions from the government, like land for new stations or the increased size of existing ones, and they prayed concerning obstructions to the mission work. Ivor's training under Rees Howells at the Bible College of Wales had convinced him of the power of prayer as an essential weapon in the work. His family in Wales prayed for him regularly and he saw direct answers as a consequence, such as his ability to overcome his fear of wild life like snakes.

The first conference was held in July, with missionaries attending from all the HAM stations. Everyone looked forward to the annual gathering. There was much news to catch up on, the long distances between stations preventing many from seeing their colleagues since the conference of the year before. The new missionary recruits, including Ivor and Rose, who had arrived in the Congo during the year, were warmly welcomed by the experienced team. The missionary conference was a huge success, a special time of refreshing their relationship with the Lord and receiving new vision for the work. The prayer and praise were so inspiring that everyone was very reluctant to bring the conference to a close.

Afterwards Ivor and Eric again plunged into the heavy workload of preparing for the Congolese Christians' conference at Christmas. Their plans included the construction of at least six wooden accommodation sheds, each 25 by eight metres, designed to hold 500 people each. At first 100 men worked on them, with the number growing to 250.

They needed thousands of poles, much of it mahogany that was plentiful in the area, as well as masses of elephant grass, bamboo, roofing grass, and rope. Men went out in the forest every day to cut and carry in the materials, while others did the building. Other workers constructed doors, windows, tables, chairs, boxes, and floor boards.

In addition, every Wednesday between 50 and 80 local Christian men gave a day to work on the church. On Thursdays, it was the women's turn. The hope was that the 70 by 30 metres open-sided structure would accommodate 10,000 people. It was built by erecting poles in long parallel lines with bamboo tied along the tops of them. Over the lengths of bamboo were tied thousands of palm branches which provided shade for the congregation.

Again, as in the previous year, the missionaries were warned that holding a huge gathering of thousands of people from diverse tribes and clans would result in clashes between them. The missionaries trusted that would not happen, investing months of prayer into the occasion. The common denominator among the tribes was their love of Christ. When the crowds began arriving it was evident that each tribal area was represented by an even greater number of people than the previous year. Some groups walked for a month to attend, covering more than 300 kilometres.

The sound of the prayer drum on the first day of the conference triggered a mighty rush to squeeze into the church building. Some missionaries sat on a platform at one end, while others mingled among the people, and another team gathered in the brick house to pray during the meetings. The Saturday meeting filled the building to capacity but an even larger number, including many non-Christian spectators, turned out on Sunday. Conservative estimates put the total number at 10,000.

Harri and his colleagues were overjoyed with the spirit of the meetings. In spite of the tremendous number the crowds were never unruly. Complete silence and perfect reverence during prayers, and attentiveness and responsiveness to the messages demonstrated the powerful presence God. The missionaries were awed at the scenes before them – the crowds, the beaming faces, the eagerness, the singing, the roars of hallelujahs. They long remembered the multitudes dispersing after each meeting – the perfect stillness during the benediction, followed by a brief pause, and then the thousands standing to their feet. African-like, they carried their small stools and chairs above their heads as they left, looking like a great waving forest of arms.

At night, inside the sleeping houses, every available inch was packed tight with human beings. Outside, hundreds of little fires peeped out of the dark, surrounded by groups of people. Often they sang and prayed into the night. In one shed the people would be singing a hymn quite different from the people in the next shed, with many tunes sung at the same time. The whole station night and day vibrated with prayers and praises.

At the conclusion people returned to their villages, challenged by the messages they had heard. Messages made it clear that everyone wanting to serve the Lord needed the in-filling of the Holy Spirit and could not be half-hearted about their faith. For some the challenge of measuring up to God's standards was too great and they chose to withdraw from the church. However, as the result of the conference, many were built up in their faith and encouraged to persevere.

[1] Heart of Africa Mission, HAM, was the name given to the mission in 1913. In 1919 the name was changed to Worldwide Evangelisation Crusade, allowing for the inclusion of service in other parts of the world, other than Africa. The name Heart of Africa Mission continued to be used in reference to the Congo for some years after 1919.

[2] Most new missionaries to the Congo suffered from one of the tropical sicknesses, such as malaria and yellow fever, which took a toll on their energy and good health. Some were laid low for a time, others were forced to return home, and some even died.

[3] The old Kingwana language, an adulterated version of Swahili, is no longer in use.

11

Bwana Kumi and Mama Kumi

Nineteen thirty-five was a significant year for the mission and for Ivor and Rose. In April 1935 the Bible school for indigenous Christians opened and, in September, Ivor Davies married Rose Sore.

Several serious stumbling blocks to future development came into clear focus in 1934. Amid an increasing number of calls from new converts for teachers of the Bible it became obvious that the Congolese evangelists were not adequate for the task. They had a limited understanding of the gospel message and yet they were asked to explain it to others. CT Studd had recognised the problem years earlier and had spoken about establishing a Bible school to give the evangelists a comprehensive understanding of the scriptures.

Despite an initial lack of funds or time to plan such an immense undertaking Harri knew it was essential to take the initiative and establish a school as soon as possible. The future of the gospel in the Congo depended upon the move. There would never be enough missionaries and the bulk of the work must be undertaken by indigenous evangelists belonging to an indigenous church, able to stand on its own feet when the missionaries departed. To succeed, an autonomous ethnic church needed its own leaders, trained in the Word of God.

Standing in the way of the Bible school was another major problem – illiteracy. It was almost universal among the Congolese, apart from the missionary-taught pastors and evangelists and employees in government agencies. Widespread illiteracy resulted in some converts doing strange things in their ignorance, like using the Bible as a talisman to ward away thieves in their homes, or pressing it against their bodies to heal ailments.

Harri knew the Bible school would be a failure without simultaneously addressing the problem of illiteracy. How could new evangelists grasp the nuances of scripture if they could barely read it? Village church leaders who could not read and were therefore unable to grasp the spirit of the gospel would create problems among those they were pastoring.

Although the missionaries had more than enough work to cope with, both the illiteracy problem and the Bible school became top priorities. In 1934 Ivor and his helpers started work on the school compound, comprising 24 bamboo Congolese houses and a brick school/kitchen building for lessons and meals. Harri wondered how the already stretched budget would cope with the building costs. However, as the work began, funds flooded in.

To confront the illiteracy problem, Harri organised Frank Cripps to print thousands of 'primer sheets' on the Ibambi press to teach villagers all over the HAM area to read and write. Frank had taught himself to run the simple treadle printing press, which in time he ingeniously rigged to be powered by a gasoline engine. He became an excellent printer, handling HAM's printing needs from New Testaments to teaching materials in various local languages.[1] Harri made a ruling that no man could be a village church leader unless he could read the Bible. The results were excellent: many thousands of Congolese adults and children learnt to read and to write their own language.

The school opened on 1 April 1935 and a circular was sent to all the mission stations calling for the missionaries to send their able converts for training. Harri warned the missionaries to send only genuine Christians who reflected their change of heart in the way they lived. They were to send both husband and wife, for it was equally important that both spouses were committed to the gospel.

Over the following two years progress in training evangelists was slow. Many had reading problems or could not cope with the simple maths they were taught. Some evangelists had strained marital relationships because their wives objected to having to sit in classes. In fact, the women cried because they had to come to school. Others were involved in tribal disagreements. At one point the high standards and demands placed on the trainees saw the numbers drop to five.

However, persistence won the day and the women wept when their course was completed and they had to leave the wonderful school environment. Ten years after opening, the school was full with 50 enthusiastic students. In another five years the school was equipped with a combined dining and meeting hall, large enough to meet the needs of 150 adults, and a number of small brick bungalows, each to house a married couple. Today the Ibambi Bible School, the main Swahili faculty, still operates, along with a secondary school.

In 1937 the decision to establish an indigenous church was unanimously agreed to by Africans and missionaries at a combined conference. Each grouping of churches around a mission station formed a diocese, with oversight vested in its own leaders. An elected Congolese overseer considered candidates for baptism, handled problems, and oversaw the 'offerings' made in the area.

For a year and a half Ivor and Rose worked alongside each other at the Ibambi Station, Rose busy with the medical work, and Ivor in the construction of new buildings. Ivor saw several engaged missionary couples arrive at the station, some of the bridegrooms sharing his room overnight on route to Uganda to be married. He occasionally wondered whether or not it would soon be his turn to find a marriage partner. If he had his eye on Rose he must have felt his hopes dashed when in mid-1933 she became engaged to another missionary. However, that relationship foundered and came to an end.

The following year Ivor and Rose announced their engagement. Years later, Ivor said that it suddenly came to both Rose and himself, while they were apart, that they were meant for one another. The Lord brought them together. Ivor did not engineer it and neither did Rose, but the Lord revealed it in such a way that they had no doubt about it at all.

Ivor was building a brick church at Niangara, some distance north of Ibambi, at the time of their decision to marry. Because of a HAM ruling that missionaries had to be involved in the work for at least two years prior to their marriage Ivor and Roses' big day was deferred and, in the interim, Rose moved to Badua to work among the Balika tribe.

British citizens found it difficult to marry in the Belgian Congo, for British law made it impossible to get married without going to Leopoldville,[2] hundreds of kilometres away. The alternative was to get the correct papers from London but that was an expensive process. Harri sent couples to Uganda, a British colony, which had the same conditions for marriage as England, and was a cheaper option than a marriage in the Congo, even taking into account the travel to and from Uganda.

Ivor and Rose carefully considered their decision to marry. They wanted ample time to test their fellowship before the Lord and to know for certain if it was the Lord's will and if the work they were called to would benefit if they got married. On the other hand they looked forward to working hand-in-hand, to helping each other and to sharing a prayer partnership.

It was not a light matter to think of marriage as a way of 'helping each other' and being in 'prayer partnership'. Some missionary couples lived alone on very isolated mission stations. One couple, married just eighteen months, departed with their six-month-old baby to a distant outpost where they worked for more than a year without seeing another European. Under such circumstances relationships needed to be resilient and robust.

Ivor and Rose, accompanied by another engaged couple, May Thorburn and Vernon Willson, another of the 1932 Ten, made the arduous journey by road to Arua in the Upper Nile District of Uganda. On 13 September 1935 they were married in Arua's Emmanuel Anglican Church by Canon Voller, who worked for the Africa Inland Mission. Ma Mupanda, as Rose was first called, became Ma or Mama Kumi.

They would spend the next 50 years together, forming a strong relationship that stood the test of lengthy separations for the sake of their ministry. Rose did not enjoy the limelight but became a solid mainstay of all they achieved, an integral part of the team. Not one to be easily swayed she was an independent thinker with her own opinions, able to say, "we agree to differ". She was wise yet down to earth, practical and spiritual, biblically knowledgeable and an effective speaker.

[1] Janet & Geoff Benge, *Norman Grubb: Mission Builder*, page 175.

[2] Leopoldville was the capital of the Belgian Congo. In 1966 it was renamed Kinshasa, having become the capital of the Democratic Republic of the Congo. With a population of 15 million in 2021 it is the most populous city in Africa.

12

A New Life in Opienge

For Ivor and Rose marriage introduced a new life in a new area, that of Opienge. It was a region with an interesting story.

In the spring of 1931 a strange and unexpected sight confronted a Congolese tribe in the remote Ituri Forest, the world's second largest rain forest. Into their village down a narrow path limped a diminutive Congolese foreigner from the far north, alone except for his wife following behind. The villagers must have wondered if their surprise visitor was in his right mind, because for generations the visitors' tribe and the Balumbi tribe in the Ituri Forest had been arch enemies, fighting each other and practising cannibalism. Now they watched one of the enemy walk into their village of his own free will.

The northern man was Zamu, a Christian converted by HAM missionaries working near his home of Nebobongo, just north of Ibambi. In 1931 a vision from God inspired Zamu to take the gospel to the southern tribes deep in the great Congo Basin. Apart from the obvious danger the 300-kilometre trek was no mean undertaking, as he was lame, with a large ulcerous wound on one leg that had failed to respond to medical treatment. As a result he limped on the toes of one foot.

Zamu had a reputation as a fiery man of prayer and an advocate of the gospel in the villages of his tribe. When he took his proposal to trek south to Esme Roupell, the HAM missionary who lived near his own village, she pointed out the dangers of the journey, testing his resolve. Was he not putting his life at risk by going among a foreign tribe without a white missionary? What about the difficulties of walking so far on a lame leg? Might he not starve? What about his wife?

"God is, White Lady," Zamu simply stated in answer to each question, feeling that was a satisfactory reply.

Initially the Balumbi people treated Zamu well, a curiosity more than anything else. They had never before seen a person like him, so void of the usual vices of drinking, gambling, fighting and immorality. He did not want to take advantage of anyone, nor did he expect to be treated as an important individual.

However, the relationship soured when the stray man began to preach a message that highlighted the wrongs of their lifestyle. Without the generosity of a chief's brother, who received Zamu's message of God's salvation, the two visitors would have starved.

Soon other members of Zamu's home church appeared to help share the gospel with the Balumbi, and then two missionaries, Jim and Ida Grainger, arrived to establish a mission station nearby at Opienge. Zamu's trek sparked a missionary spirit in the indigenous church and African Christians began moving in different directions to preach the gospel to other tribes.

Four years later Ivor and Rose followed in Zamu's footsteps. The confetti had barely settled when the newly-weds set off from Ibambi for the isolated depths of the Ituri Forest and their new home, the Opienge Station. The Davies assumed responsibility for Opienge, enabling the Graingers to establish a new station at Lubutu, 200 kilometres to the southwest.

Opienge was world-renowned in naturalist circles as the home of a small rare and endangered animal, the okapi, related to the giraffe family. Most missionaries, however, associated the area with its notorious road. The journey from Ibambi to Opienge began on the main Stanleyville[1] Road beyond Bafwasende, a good dry-season road, except for the clouds of red dust behind the missionary trucks, which penetrated and coated everything including the passengers. Travel in the wet season was a different matter. Regular tropical storms cut deep gullies across the road in unexpected places, causing drivers to brake frequently to avoid serious impairment to their vehicles. Suspension damage was common, as were makeshift repairs on the road.

However, that road paled into insignificance compared to the second half of the journey – Angumu Road, the access to Opienge, one of the worst the missionaries encountered. That treacherous road was originally constructed for the government to service the Angumu Gold Mines, 80 kilometres beyond the Opienge Station. Travellers to Opienge had to drive 110 kilometres through thick forest along what was little more than a muddy track, deeply rutted by heavy vehicles from the gold mines.

The road had countless hairpin bends and some 72 bridges, with streams and rivers requiring repeated crossing and recrossing. The 'bridges' consisted of little more than planks tied to felled trees and rolled into position. Some wondered if the government's payment to the road builders on a per kilometre basis encouraged its convoluted excessive length. On alternate days traffic was permitted to travel in one direction only, except on Sundays, when vehicles could go both ways. Only the bravest traveller would then risk meeting a vehicle coming in the opposite direction, for there were few places to pass.

Ivor and Rose's first journey to Opienge, twenty kilometres north of the equator, was incident free, but they felt the full impact of their new location and its isolation as the driver of the lurching missionary truck transported them further and further into the wild virgin forest. Near the end of their journey the road rose steeply. Around yet another bend and the Opienge station finally came into view, down in a valley running away at right angles from the road. Mud and bamboo buildings that served as missionary accommodation, a boys' school, and a church stood on a flat area near the road. Congolese accommodation and vegetable gardens could be seen further up the valley. Surrounding the station was wild, forested and mountainous terrain.

Opienge was indeed very remote. Unlike other HAM stations, which were 40 to 80 kilometres apart from each other, the new home of Ivor and Rose was 250 kilometres from the nearest station. The closest town with a doctor and shops was Stanleyville, 360 kilometres away. They had no car and, as the Angumu Road was a dead-end beyond the gold mines, the only regular passing traffic were trucks belonging to the mine. No other Europeans lived near Opienge and just a few Belgians were stationed at the mines 80 kilometres away.

In the 1930s the only way of contacting other stations was via the fortnightly mail service, with radio-telephone technology a thing of the future. Internal mail was very slow, with a letter mailed to Britain reaching its destination before a letter posted to Ibambi. In an emergency there was no way to summon immediate help.

Ivor and Rose were limited by language barriers, because Kingwana, which they used to communicate with tribes in the north, was virtually unknown among the Balumbi. Consequently they had to learn the Congo-Swahili trade language of the Opienge district.

One huge blessing in their new work was veteran missionary, Esme Roupell, with her great depth of experience. Since her arrival in the Congo in 1916, in the days of CT Studd, she had worked in many areas. While others assisted from time to time at Opienge, Esme, Ivor and Rose formed the permanent staff after the departure of the Graingers.

Ivor and Rose were much impressed by the forest surrounding the Opienge station. Everything grew prolifically, colourfully and to mammoth proportions. Trees with massive trunks developed to 50 metres or more, their branchy crowns forming a canopy which denied the forest floor all but a little sunlight. Lianas, creeping vines which throttled trees, hung from the tree tops, bursting into blossoms of blue, purple, yellow and crimson where they found sufficient sunlight. The Ituri Forest had tens of thousands of endemic trees and plants, animals, birds, and insects, many of which remain unidentified or named, even today. Wild animals in the Opienge region included elephants, buffaloes, baboons and gorillas, as well as the rare okapi.

The forest was also home to the pygmy people, a diminutive race of itinerant hunters and gatherers who avoided unnecessary contact with the village-dwelling Congolese and other foreigners. The pygmies used their tiny bows, poisoned arrows and nets to hunt game and to fish the rivers. In addition, they ate fruits and roots. They set up their forest camps wherever the hunting was best. If they caught an elephant and killed it, they would establish a little pygmy camp nearby in a matter of hours.

While the pygmies relied on the forest for their livelihood the village-dwelling Congolese fought a relentless battle against it, the vegetation constantly threatening to encroach on the land they had cleared for food crops. The Opienge region was a particularly difficult area for arable farmers to eke out a living. The poor white sandy soils produced relatively small and undependable crop yields and the area was well removed from produce markets. Poor transportation and bad roads made it all the more difficult for the farmers to make a good living. The close proximity of virgin forest meant baboons and elephants invaded the vegetable gardens at night, inflicting damage and loss of production, sometimes causing farmers to go hungry.

However, wild animals also provided food for the local villagers who regularly hunted in the forest with spears and other weapons. Sometimes they offered game to the missionaries who gratefully accepted it, as their only regular meat came from the chickens, ducks, rabbits, pigeons and goats kept on the station. But Ivor and Rose learned the wisdom of asking the hunters how far away the 'kill' had been made before accepting meat. In the tropical heat and humidity fresh meat quickly deteriorated, sometimes arriving at Opienge after swinging on the shoulder of a rainforest porter for several days.

Despite the poverty of the local population they were tremendously generous at times, considering their circumstances. The Balumbi often gave away the first fruits of their gardens, whether it was maize, peanuts or rice. They would approach Rose with a bowlful for herself or for the 'box of God'.

Although the rare okapi and gorillas lived in the Opienge region the missionaries rarely saw them in the wild, as they lived deep in the forest. Once, while Ivor was trekking to some villages, he passed by the Angumu Gold Mines and had an opportunity to see animals being held in captivity, on their way to zoos in London, New York and Brussels.

Life in the jungle brought all sort of surprises. The Opienge missionaries became accustomed to being awakened abruptly in the middle of the night by screaming chimpanzees that came right up to their house. Sometimes Ivor ventured outside, hoping to scare them away.

There was plenty to do on the station – teaching in the boys' school, pastoring the small church of Congolese Christians, working in the medical clinic, constructing new buildings and visiting neighboring villages. When Ivor cycled into a village, smiling and singing at the top of his voice in Welsh, his arrival usually created an uproar, for white men were still rare in the southern Ituri Forest. During the school holiday breaks Ivor and several Congolese helpers travelled his area of responsibility, a region 200 kilometres long and 100 wide, sharing Jesus with those who had yet to receive the gospel.

Though Jim and Ida Grainger had visited many villages during their time at Opienge Ivor encountered a number, particularly in the south, that had never seen a white man or a missionary. Several mission organisations worked in the Belgian Congo by the 1930s but none had penetrated the region surrounding Opienge. Prior to Zamu's and the Graingers' arrival, there had been no Christian witness within ten days walking distance of the Opienge station.

In their early days Rose accompanied Ivor on treks. After their first child Ioan was born in 1936 Congolese porters, who had tremendous stamina, transported the baby in a sedan chair, along with other luggage, for hour after hour. Trekking was not for the faint-hearted. Though little sunlight penetrated the thick forest canopy, the environment was hot and sticky, in close proximity to the equator. Undergrowth quickly overgrew forest paths, the man at the front of the party hacking it away as he went. The risk of disease, wild animals or belligerent locals was real, but that never stopped even the single women missionaries from travelling alone, with perhaps one or two Congolese assistants, into the furthest corners of the mission area.

Ivor did not suffer any serious injuries from animals though he had his share of close encounters. One day he and several African Christians were crossing the Ituri River by canoe when they noticed the water swirling in an odd manner a few metres away. Suddenly a large crocodile surfaced, heading straight for the vessel.

"Paddle for your life," Ivor cried out. Despite frantic paddling, the crocodile gained on the canoe. As it drew up alongside one of the Congolese men thumped the crocodile on its head with his paddle. The whack momentarily stunned the reptile but it soon resumed the chase. Just in time, the paddlers reached the safety of the shore, their hearts pounding with relief.

On the return journey through the forest, later that same day, there was more trouble. The group made its way in the darkness, only a kerosene lamp illuminating the path, when suddenly they detected huge elephant footprints. Soon they heard the roar of elephant trumpets a short distance away. The disturbed elephants began to follow the men, who froze with fear, aware of the extreme danger of the wild animals. They also knew it was futile to run, for the elephants were far too swift.

"Let's pray, Bwana," one man suggested, and they all mouthed desperate hurried prayers.

Then they loudly struck up the song Ku Jina Ya Yesu (In the name of Jesus), which echoed through the forest. When the song finished there was silence, and they realised the elephants had disappeared. Their relief was immense.

[1] Stanleyville was renamed Kisangani in 1966.

13

Seeking Followers of Jesus

To find the most effective method of presenting the gospel Ivor had to feel his way. Often people were unable to read or write and it was difficult to give them an understanding of the meaning of the gospel story. One village they visited time and again but failed to have any impact. At least 200 people came and listened and yet they seemed to have little understanding. The missionaries prayed about the area, and Ivor preached as well as he could, but there was no response.

One evening, after speaking to the villagers without result, Ivor sat down beside his glowing storm lantern, despondently watching the insects buzzing around the light. The people's attention switched from Ivor to a Congolese storyteller who began to entertain them. Storytelling was a popular pastime and they spent hours entertaining one another with their stories. As Ivor considered his next move he became aware on his right of two villagers ignoring the storyteller. Instead they engaged in a heated conversation of their own about another man.

He was a terrible person who had stolen a goat. "We would never do that," they said. Ivor wondered how they knew stealing was wrong. He joined their conversation, asking them the question. They looked at him with great surprise.

"We all know that," they replied. Ivor asked them who told them stealing was wrong. Soon others noticed Ivor in conversation with them and they crowded around to listen.

"We've always known that it's wrong because our fathers told us," one replied.

"Who told your fathers?" Ivor asked.

"Their fathers and . . . the chiefs," they replied.

Ivor persisted. "All right, but who told your fathers' fathers and the chiefs?"

"We've just always known that it's wrong!" they stubbornly answered.

"If stealing is wrong, what about adultery? Is that wrong too?"

"Yes, of course," they agreed.

"How do you know?" he asked.

"Because it just is!" they replied again.

"What's the penalty?" he asked, already knowing their answer.

"Death," they said. Ivor looked around at their faces.

"And who made that law?" They could not answer.

"Is killing wrong?" Ivor continued. They considered it a while before answering.

"If we go to war against another tribe it is not wrong, but if we kill one another it is."

"So," Ivor said, ticking the items off on his fingers, "you say stealing is wrong, adultery is wrong, murder is wrong. I still want to know who told you!"

"Look, white man," they said with a shrug, "you keep asking us that question but we don't know, except that it came from our fathers. We don't know where it came from in the first place."

"I can tell you," Ivor said smiling. "It is God who tells us that these things are wrong."

"God?" they said with surprise. "Does he really tell us these things?"

"Yes, he tells us we must not steal, we must not commit adultery, and we are not supposed to murder." Ivor had their undivided attention. "If we do these things punishment will come."

"Punishment?" one said with an uncomfortable tone of voice. "We haven't heard that before."

"Nevertheless it is true," Ivor continued. "God has put it in the heart of every man to know what is good and evil. If you know that it is wrong to steal and then you steal, you are guilty. Now, you condemned that man for stealing a goat. Have any of you here stolen as well? You know the penalty for adultery is death. Have any of you committed adultery?" There was silence. "What about murder? You've told me others have done it and it's wrong and yet, if you've done it yourselves, you are guilty."

When they heard that they all began to speak in Kilumbi. The discussion to that point had been in the Congo-Swahili language. They talked and talked. When they had finished their discussion one of them spoke.

"If it is true what you say, we are all guilty. But we are asking you now, can we make a pact with God? When we go to war with another tribe, and we tire of fighting, we sit the two chiefs down, kill a chicken or goat and sprinkle the blood on the two chiefs. We then cut through both of the chiefs' skins and mix their two bloods. We say the two chiefs are blood brothers and there is no more fighting. If we kill an animal will God accept its blood as a sacrifice?"

Ivor was amazed at what the man said. "There was once a time," he said, "when God accepted an animal, but not now."

"Then what is going to happen to us?" they asked.

Ivor replied, "God himself has provided a sacrifice, his own son Jesus, whom he called the Lamb. That's the reason he won't accept your sacrifice. But Jesus came and said that God hates sin but he loves the world. If you believe in him you won't be punished." They asked him when that had happened and he replied that it was a long time ago.

"Why haven't we been told this before?" they asked.

"Because people haven't come to tell you, but now I have."

"Tell us again!" they exclaimed.

Next morning Ivor had to repeat the story again. When he finished he sat down and wondered what would happen next. Much later in the day there was a response. A young man came up to Ivor and asked him whether what he had said was true or not. Ivor told him it was true.

"What do I have to do then?" he enquired.

"If you believe, you just tell God. Speak the words," Ivor told him. The young man looked puzzled.

Ivor explained. "Even though you can't see God, you can still speak to Him. He can hear what is going on right now." The young man asked Ivor how he had come to know God and Ivor told him a little of his own spiritual journey.

"Can I do it now?" he asked again. The young man followed Ivor in a simple prayer.

"Is that all?"

"Yes," Ivor replied, "that's all, but you must believe that God hears you and that you are now his."

"Anything else I need to do?" he persisted, fishing for something more tangible to confirm his new faith.

"Go to those men over there and tell them what you've just done," Ivor told him. Shortly afterwards Ivor had several people around him with heads bowed in prayer.

Preaching and witnessing to the gospel in the villages was not an easy task. Normal life continued around the missionaries as they spoke. An argument could well begin in the middle of Ivor's address to a gathered group. The gospel message was spread in a variety of ways and sometimes as the result of unusual occurrences. Ivor discovered people in villages who had experienced dreams prior to his arrival. Some listened quietly for days or even months to what he had to say before they made a commitment. Then they told him it was a dream that had made them listen to him in the first place.

Others went on a journey, turning up where the missionaries were, and then returned to their homes to tell their folk what had happened. When the children went back to their villages from the mission schools they took the Bible stories with them. They read the stories aloud and the village gathered around to listen to the gospel.

Part of the struggle was convincing the people that Christianity was more powerful than witchcraft, but when the Congolese saw paralysed people healed and released through prayer many turned to the Lord.

14

Mission Station at Work

A Medical Centre

When Ivor and Rose arrived at Opienge medicines and treatment were completely unavailable. The urgent need for a medical centre was therefore obvious, but Rose needed to win the confidence of the women to dispense her expertise and basic medicines. While the village men were approachable the women were extremely shy, reluctant to talk and unwilling to accept medical treatment. After Rose tried several approaches the answer came in a very natural way.

On 28 August 1936 Ioan Davies, Ivor and Rose's first child, was born. When the family arrived back at Opienge from Ibambi with little Ioan the barriers between the local women and Rose disappeared. The shared experience of childbirth was the key. The mothers crowded around the new arrival, anxious to catch a glimpse of the first white baby many of them had seen. It was the culmination of interest shown in Rose over the previous months, with excitement mounting as the date for her baby's birth drew near. Rose's pre-breakfast clinic became well patronised as news spread concerning the benefits of the white woman's treatment.

The women customarily helped each other with childbirth but began summoning Rose in the event of a problem. Calls also came for help when a villager was bitten by a snake or caught under a falling tree. Sometimes Rose had to walk several kilometres to a village, even in the middle of the night.

At times Rose's skills could not save the life of a mother during childbirth but if the baby lived, she made sure it was properly fostered, bringing little ones back to the station. She did not raise them as white children, housing them in their own home, putting them in their children's beds or letting them eat what they ate. Such actions would have led to difficulties in the future, with the children having trouble adapting to the African way of life when they were older.

Rose brought a woman or mature girl with the baby who was willing to care for the little one, though finding someone was not always easy. Because the Congolese were afraid of witchcraft and curses, and suspected that was the reason why the mother had died, they were reluctant to look after the baby for fear he or she was cursed as well. Consequently the carers were usually Christian women, coming onto the mission compound where they were given a house in which to look after the child.

Hand-in-hand with medical treatment was a need for health education. The older midwives were slower to change their ways, their methods sometimes causing infant deaths at birth. The younger Christian women were quicker to employ better birthing ways, realising that mortality rates improved when they adopted Rose's methods. Esme and Rose gave basic hygiene classes, outlining ways of avoiding infections. While the Congolese practised good bodily hygiene, washing nearly their whole body twice a day, they needed instruction for the proper care of sores and wounds and for ways to avoid food contamination.

Schooling for Girls

As they preached around the villages the missionaries found girls who wanted to go to school but whose parents were opposed to the idea. One ten-year-old girl, in particular, persistently raised questions about the Bible and her desire to read. Ivor discussed it with Rose and Esme, wanting to do something for her, but recognising there was much antagonism in the tribe against teaching girls.

Because the girl's mother was a Christian she allowed her to come to the station accompanied by a friend, to stay with Esme in her home. Esme began to teach them in a casual fashion in her house and soon six or seven other girls came to the station, wanting to learn. Not long after, their parents arrived demanding that the girls be handed back. The missionaries said the girls had come to the station voluntarily to learn, but the parents replied that girls were not supposed to learn.

"Girls are just play things," they said. "They are just like dogs. You don't teach dogs such things."

"My wife and Miss Roupell have both learned to read," Ivor responded.

"Oh, but they are white," they replied.

"Look," Ivor said, "just listen to this young girl read," and he encouraged one of the girls to read a few lines to them. The people were amazed. She could actually read. When more and more girls arrived in the hope of being schooled Ivor had a girls' school and a dormitory built to house them and gardens planted to provide food for the boarders.

An eleven-year-old girl did very well but her parents wanted her married and took her away. The man who was to marry her had paid the dowry and her parents wanted the girl to start going to his village to become accustomed to him. However, the girl ran back to the mission, rushing into the Davies' bedroom, terrified of her pursuing parents. Ivor was outside when the group of eight villagers arrived, including the girl's grandparents. Workmen and others gathered around to witness the drama.

"It's not a bad thing for your girl to be taught to read," Ivor said to the parents. "Would you allow us to keep her here?" They refused, and wanted her to go with them.

"Why is it that you want young girls to come onto the station?" they asked. It was a revealing question.

"You have your own wife and the other lady as well." They obviously believed Esme was Ivor's second wife.

"Is it because you want to gather women around you?" they asked. Ivor began to understand their thinking.

"What you say is not true," he replied. "You can ask anyone living on the compound and they will tell you."

The girl's mother, naked from the waist – as the local women were – grew hysterical, shaking and throwing her arms in the air. Screaming wildly she threatened to take her life with the small dull rusty gardening knife she had strapped to her hip. With a flash of intuition Ivor offered her his own shiny pocket knife. The gathered crowd began to laugh.

"Bwana is harmless, see," they said.

The incident proved a turning point. Those present told other parents Ivor was harmless and they began to understand the missionaries were not out to exploit the girls by making them work or by adding them as wives. The result was they allowed their daughters to go to school.

Other inquisitive minds asked the girls searching questions when they began boarding with Esme. Because polygamy had been practised in the culture for generations they naturally assumed Ivor had two wives, despite the fact that Esme lived in her own house. Enquirers wanted to know when Bwana Kumi made his nocturnal visits to Esme and were most bemused when the girls reported that Ivor never made such visits.

Other Schooling Challenges

The three Opienge missionaries were not trained teachers. In fact, Ivor and Rose had received schooling up to only thirteen or fourteen years of age but they counted that as an advantage. Because of the struggles Ivor in particular had experienced he felt he could better understand his pupils' learning difficulties.

Initial attempts to teach the children the alphabet proved fruitless, for it made little sense to them. Soon the tutors struck upon the idea of teaching them in a phonetic manner, starting with words most familiar to the children, like 'mama or baba'. By linking together the two simple syllables of each word the children began to understand the mechanics of their language and to read fluently.

As they learnt how to read and write in Swahili they enquired about farming methods. The government wanted the Congolese to plant cotton and peanuts in rows, rather than all over the place. The men normally pushed a hole in the ground with a stick and the women came behind, shoving the seed in with their toes. The missionaries taught them to make furrows using a stick, with a cord to get a straight line, according to government wishes. They also obtained books about cotton diseases and began to instruct them about pests like weevils.

At one stage, Ivor had 80 boys in his school and Esme had 50 girls, all of whom were living on the station compound. The students returned to their parents' villages for the school holidays but there was no guarantee they would come back to the mission afterwards. The parents in the early days rarely compelled their children to attend, with the children pleasing themselves. Neither was there government compulsion for the Congolese to attend the protestant mission schools. In fact, it was rather the contrary.

Until 1925 the only attempt to educate the Africans was made by the protestant missions. However, in the wake of a visit to the country by Vatican representatives a law was passed stating the Roman Catholic Church should be the only educating body in the country. From 1925 to 1948 government subsidies were given to Catholic schools, enabling them to establish a number of large, well-equipped schools around the country, including eventually in the Opienge district.

After 1948 a liberal government made subsidies available to the many protestant schools operating in the country. Some missions accepted them, but HAM did not because of dissatisfaction with some of the requirements. For example, the school buildings had to meet specified standards, and teachers had to be fully qualified in order to receive the 100 percent salary subsidy. In addition, the government did not look favourably on boarding schools like those on the stations.

The subsidy question was a contentious one. When a mission did not avail itself of the advantages in the subsidy system students were likely to be later disadvantaged in state examinations. Eventually the mission felt it necessary to send the more promising students to other stations for secondary education or training in the Ibambi Bible School. Others were sent back to the villages after two or three years in the Opienge schools, where they themselves taught basic reading and writing skills to others and worked as evangelists. The 'bush schools' resulted in hundreds more young people becoming literate.

Family Life

"Bwana, why do you quarrel so much with your family?" a helper asked Ivor one day while they were working on a station building.

"Quarrel?" responded Ivor. "What do you mean, 'quarrel'?"

"Whenever you talk to your family in that strange language it sounds like you are arguing with them – telling them off," said the man.

Ivor was familiar with the accusation. They considered the English language sounded harsh and, because they did not understand what was being said, they wondered if unkind words were being spoken. Ivor reassured them by translating the conversation. They laughed and said it was a funny language.

There was little privacy in family life. Virtually everything they did was subjected to scrutiny and comment. Because of the missionaries' heavy workload, they had Congolese gardeners, house cleaners, and cooks working for them who were always around, seeing first-hand what went on inside Bwana's home. News spread fast and anything that happened in the Davies household quickly became village knowledge. They were an open book and had to be very careful in the way they spoke and did things, trying to live a life of goodness and gentleness, and rebuking in a spirit tempered with truth and honesty.

By 1943 Ioan had two sisters and a brother. Miriam was born in 1938, Evan in 1940, followed three years later by Megan. As in any normal family the Davies' children had to be disciplined from time to time.

On occasions they had to explain to the locals how and why they corrected their children. The indigenous people largely allowed their children to do what they liked until they became so annoyed that they suddenly picked up a stick or axe, beating the child with it. They did not understand how to sit a child down and reason with him or her. Sometimes the missionaries intervened and tried to explain better methods. They also introduced classes to teach parenting skills, showing them scriptures and explaining it was right to correct their children, but also necessary to tell them why.

A Choir for Opienge

The Davies children enjoyed a rich musical heritage from their father and loved singing together. Ivor had only one musical record in the Congo, the *Messiah*, which he loved. So much so that he sang his children to sleep by singing the Hallelujah Chorus!

Teaching the school children to sing took patience and effort.

"Doh Ray Me Fah Soh Lah Te Doh!" rang out the sound of the musical scale in the class room. Then it was followed by "Come on, stop your laughing. Altogether now," said Ivor as he attempted without much success to conduct a singing lesson.

Every time he sang "Doh, Me, Soh, Doh, Me, Soh, Doh", it was accompanied by raucous laughter. He could not figure out why. Finally he pulled a boy aside and asked why they were laughing. The boy reluctantly confided that 'Doh Me' sounded like the word in the Kilumbi language for 'starch' and 'Oh' sounded like the word for stomach. When Ivor sang 'oooooooooh', going up and down the scale, it indicated he had a sore stomach!

Once Ivor had cleared that misunderstanding it was back to the serious business of teaching singing. And sing they would. His reputation as a Welshman was on the line. If anyone could teach people to sing it was a Welshman. On his arrival in the Congo Ivor found the usual practice was for the missionary leading the service to sing a line of a hymn which the congregation then repeated. To a man accustomed to the four-part harmonies of Welsh congregations it was an appalling state of affairs, one he set out to rectify.

He knew the Congolese could harmonise because he heard them during their dances and it frustrated him to hear them repeating words line by line. Ivor wrote a very simple tune on the board and asked his pupils to repeat it until they knew it off by heart. Soon they realised they were singing a familiar hymn without using the words. Ivor then taught them the alto harmony, next splitting the choir into two. When they sang the two parts together they were amazed at the result. In time he had them singing in four-part harmony, and was delighted to find them singing together at work in their gardens or enjoying themselves at night. His success with the choir brought him great satisfaction.

Church Growth

The aim of every HAM missionary was to establish indigenous churches in the villages. Ivor had overall responsibility for 40 small village churches, with several of them under the pastoral leadership of individual Bible school trainees from Ibambi, assisted by Opienge school students. In 1937 the Congolese church began sending out its own paid evangelists, and in 1940 they voluntarily assumed responsibility for financing the Ibambi Bible School. The demand for training facilities continued to increase, necessitating the establishment of three other Bible schools.

It was a proud day for the Opienge missionaries when, after much hard work, their first candidates headed off to begin training at Ibambi. Literacy levels had lifted to a point where they were now ready to take advantage of more in-depth Bible study.

Another church growth goal was to encourage the indigenous church to tithe and support their own workers, for reliance on overseas funding discouraged them from taking responsibility for their own personnel. A basket was placed in front of the church for items like eggs, rice, and corn-on-the-cob which the missionaries purchased, turning the money over to the church. At harvest time the people were taught to give a tenth of their produce to the Lord's work, bringing the money they received at the markets back to the church.

At first, the money was sent to Ibambi, where they divided it up and gave it to the evangelists. But the pool system was very impersonal and did not teach them direct responsibility for their own evangelists. When they saw their money supported their own evangelists they made their gardens a little bigger in order to give more.

One contentious issue that arose involved polygamists who became Christians. The missionaries did not pressure converts to put aside all but one wife, for it marginalised the discarded wives. However young Christian men contemplating marriage were taught God's expectations – one man, one wife. What their fathers had done in taking several wives was done in ignorance. The young men, having the benefit of the scriptural injunction, had no such excuse. There was often bitter resistance to changes in such age-old practices and sometimes converted polygamists expressed a desire to serve as church officers. But the missionaries knew from scriptures that the two were mutually exclusive, and would not allow men practising polygamy to take on church office.

In the early years during CT Studd's time in leadership new Christians were baptised by full immersion. However, problems began to arise when people believed, were baptised, and then fell into sin again. They would still want to take communion and so standards began to slip.

To counter the problem CT began classes for those serious about their faith, teaching them the need for holiness in their Christian walk. Subsequent missionaries continued the lessons, resulting in a high moral standard and commitment to God. The importance of baptism and the sacredness of the Lord's table were included in the lessons. The foundation that CT laid continued as a strength of the mission.

New Missionary

In November 1937 Ivor was overjoyed when his younger brother David arrived in the Belgian Congo, adding another member of the extended family to the HAM work, which already included Rose's sister Daisy and her husband Eric Smith.

15

War and Furlough

In September 1939 Hitler's tanks rolled into Poland in an invasion which led to World War II. In the Western World every news service carried the shocking news, but it was slow to reach those living in the heart of Africa. With delays in their fortnightly mail service invasion announcements did not reach Ivor and Rose until a month after the event.

When Britain declared war on Germany the sense of isolation intensified. There was a degree of irony in the new situation, for in the past the missionaries were the ones living in a potentially hostile environment, giving their families cause for concern. Now people at home in Britain were the ones in greater peril.

Communication problems increased. Merchant ships carrying mail were frequently sunk or delayed. Missionaries were startled to hear up-to-date news from a passing trader, indicating that the Germans had advanced faster and further through Europe and North Africa. They wondered whether the Germans would over-run Britain and they worried for their families, finding it disconcerting that they could not follow the war intelligently.

The Belgian Congo, though remote from the battle fronts in Europe, was nevertheless affected by the war. The Governor vowed that the country would do all it could to free European Belgium. Expatriate Belgians and Congolese men were enlisted to fight. It seemed possible Germany might respond and take over the Belgian Congo but that did not eventuate.

Ivor and Rose were due for furlough in the early 1940s but the war prevented their return to Britain. Not only did their private mail and newspapers go down with torpedoed supply ships, but also support money. When finances failed to arrive other missionaries shared their resources with Ivor and Rose.

In early 1945, during the final stages of the war in Europe, Harri sent word to Ivor, Rose and their four children to prepare to depart. Rose's sister and brother-in-law Daisy and Eric Smith and their three children – Derek, Paul and Roy – were to accompany them. Excitement grew as hurried arrangements were made for the 1900-kilometre trip to Leopoldville to rendezvous with the ship Copacabana.

After gathering at Ibambi the two families set out on the first leg of the journey – a 400-kilometre dash in the missionary truck to Stanleyville in just a day. The Davies and Smith children found the night in their Stanleyville hotel most intriguing. Modern conveniences, such as bathroom taps with running water, were a new experience they did not have on the mission stations.

The next morning they boarded a wood-burning river steamer for the ten-day 1500- kilometre journey on the Congo River to Leopoldville. The food was good and accommodation comfortable and there was plenty of time to take in the beautiful river scenery. The relaxed atmosphere evaporated on arrival in the city, for when Ivor and Eric reported to the shipping agent, they learnt that the Copacabana had been commandeered by the government solely to repatriate Belgian citizens to their now-free homeland.

The ship departed, leaving the two missionary couples and their seven children stranded with limited resources. Rose was also in the later stages of pregnancy. Colonel Bequet, a Salvation Army officer, came to their rescue, offering the party two houses in the officers' training centre, providing them accommodation and facilities for self-catering.

Over the next month Ivor and Eric tried in vain each day to book a group passage to Britain. There was a desperate shortage of vessels due to the number of ships commandeered for the war effort and the many that had been sunk. Harri declined Ivor and Eric's suggestion for them to return, and encouraged them to keep looking for a passage.

As Rose's condition was of some concern it was decided to fly her and youngest daughter, Megan, home to Britain. In true altruistic missionary fashion Ivor resisted the temptation to travel with Rose as air travel for the whole family would have dipped deeply into the mission's cash reserves.

For the remainder of the party the situation deteriorated before it improved. Ivor developed severe stomach pains and was admitted to hospital for a few days before regaining health. Finally Colonel Bequet arrived early one morning at their accommodation with news of a boat that would collect the group from Matadi, 320 kilometres further west down the Congo River. There the group boarded the ship Lowlander, a captured Italian vessel that had made a detour from Nigeria specifically to pick them up.

The voyage was a memorable one. The children got on well with the Chinese crew, but their enjoyment of the trip was marred by tropical heat rashes. Because of the war they had to close all the cabin port holes at night for fear of emitting any light, making their cabins stiflingly hot. All were curious to hear about the war, having been cut off from information for so long, and though the crew was guarded in what they said the families were amazed to hear the things they did report.

Tremendous celebrations greeted them at the port of Tacoradi in Ghana. On 7 May 1945 Germany surrendered to the Allied Forces and victory celebrations erupted throughout Europe and in the colonies of the victorious countries. During the eight days the Lowlander was in port loading cargo the two British families enthusiastically joined in the festivities.

Despite the official end of the war in Europe the trip remained perilous. Coming up the coast of Portugal the ship was alerted to the presence of a German submarine whose crew were unaware the war had ended. Their ship had to turn into the Atlantic Ocean away from the submarine until it was made aware the war had ended and the crew gave itself up in Spain. Passage through the English Channel was also dangerous as the seaway was heavily mined. A crewman was posted in the front of the vessel to spot mines.

At the port of Hull Ivor's brother, Luther, waited at the dockside to greet the party. Their joy at returning to their homeland was lessened when they stared in disbelief at the damage suffered by the port city. The continuous stream of comments by the children, to whom everything in Britain was new and strange, brought light relief. Nine-year-old Ioan, his younger siblings – Miriam and Evan – and their three cousins, could not stop talking about the "white black people," as they called them, who scurried about the Hull wharves, lifting and wheeling cargo. Seeing European labourers was a new experience, for in the Congo, it was the Congolese who worked on the wharves.

The group travelled by train to the London headquarters of WEC, the children's eyes glued to the windows as they excitedly pointed out the sights. In contrast the adults stared in solemn unbelief at the mountains of rubble strewn everywhere in one city after another. Ivor and Rose were reunited and set off to see their extended families, meeting their in-laws for the first time and introducing their children to their grandparents. Rose safely gave birth to baby Ruth at the Bible College of Wales Hospital[1] on 23 July 1945.

Ivor and Rose were curious to discover first-hand, from people they knew well, what had taken place in Britain during the war years. They discovered they could draw only a guarded response, even from relatives. Their family did not want to talk about the war at all, rather preferring to put it behind them and get on with life. One

114

startling thing that did not require explanation was the physical effect of the stresses of war, demonstrated in young people whose hair had turned grey or white.

Food rationing was still in place and Ivor found himself, along with many others, queuing for his family's food ration. He stood in line for bananas and was surprised when he came to the front of the queue to be offered just a few unripe ones. In Africa they were accustomed to cutting down a bunch of 30 or 40 bananas at a time. In spite of the rationing and shortages everything was organised with regimental precision, with a sense of buoyancy and security among the people.

The Davies family spent three years in Britain, with Ivor spending much of the time travelling and speaking about their experiences at church meetings and in peoples' homes. His journeys gave him an overview of the general health of the Church in Britain which, despite outward appearances, seemed promising. Many of the churches, particularly in Wales, had smaller congregations than had been the case when he departed from Britain in 1932. However, the committed church members he met were brimming with expectancy, in sharp contrast to the apathetic attitude fourteen years before.

In 1946 they received the tragic news from the Congo of the sudden death of Jack Harrison.[2] At the age of 45 the field leader for the previous fourteen years had been struck down without warning by a tropical illness and was buried at Ibambi beside the grave of CT Studd. His death came as a great loss both for the mission and personally for the missionaries who had worked with him. He had been like a son to CT and had drunk deep of his spirit, according to Norman Grubb, serving a hard leadership apprenticeship of nine years under CT, at the beck and call of everyone, but learning to submit.[3]

Harri had become leader in 1931 when it seemed as if the work might falter. Instead, it grew and consolidated under his guidance through the establishment of an adult literacy campaign, the opening of the Ibambi Bible School, the formation of the indigenous church, and the development of the Ibambi printing press. The WEC work expanded to cover an area of over 4,000 square kilometres, involving seventeen tribes.[4]

Furlough enabled Ivor and Rose to carefully consider their future plans. They had a strong desire to return to Africa. Opienge held a special place in their hearts. In addition, the new HAM field leader Jack Scholes desperately needed experienced workers. However, heart-rending decisions lay between them and a return ticket, decisions that would deeply affect their immediate family.

As their Africa-bound ship pulled away from Woolwich's Royal Albert Dock on 4 March 1948 Ivor and Rose agonised over whether they had done the right thing. Before them lay the work to which they believed God had called them. Behind them were their three eldest children, from whom they would be separated for over six years and by thousands of kilometres of ocean.

The decision to leave Ioan aged eleven, Miriam aged nine, and Evan aged seven, in Britain was a difficult one, but the reason was simple. There were no education facilities for English-speaking children in the Belgian Congo. Prior to their furlough Ivor and Rose hoped that a WEC proposal to establish a school in the Congo for resident missionary children would come about. When the plan was abandoned Ivor and Rose were immensely disappointed.

Instead, in 1946 WEC set up a home, The Elms, on the east coast of Scotland in the outskirts of the seaside town of Arbroath, under Charlie and Lily Searle, former missionaries in the Belgian Congo. Its purpose was to care for the children of missionaries working for WEC worldwide, with the children attending British state schools. Ivor and Rose visited the home in Scotland, giving it much thought. They were convinced they should return to the Congo and so made the decision to take with them only their two youngest children, Megan and Ruth.

The choice to leave the three children behind was particularly difficult for Rose. Several years later, in a letter to her three eldest children, Rose wrote: "But the Lord knows it was for His work and not in any neglectful way that we left you. Certainly, if there had been any hope of schooling out here, we would have brought you all with us. It goes against the grain to shift my responsibilities onto anyone else. I have always had a very firm conviction of the responsibility of parents, and for that reason I was not too happy about leaving you all, for I had no assurance that we were right in leaving you."

So began a family separation made at great emotional cost. For six and a half years the relationship between Ioan, Miriam, and Evan and their parents was based on the contents of the latest letter and on prayer.[5] Arguments may be mounted for and against missionaries' decisions to part from their wives and children. In the end, only God can be the judge of their obedience to His call.

[1] Some of the Bible College of Wales was turned into a hospital during World War 2.

[2] Harri won the affection and admiration of all who worked with him, Congolese and European alike. The Belgian Congo Government recognised his worth in 1937, the Belgian King awarding him the decoration of Chevalier de L'Ordre de Lion. The support that HAM received from the government was largely due to the congenial relationship Harri maintained with the officials who saw the positive impact of the mission work on the Congolese. Norman Grubb recorded Jack's story in *Successor to C. T. Studd*.

[3] Helen Roseveare, *Living Stones*, page 50.

[4] Evan Davies, *Whatever happened to CT Studd's mission?* page 45.

[5] They were not alone in their separation. Many missionary families made similar sacrifices for the sake of their work, not the least the mission's founders. CT Studd left his wife Priscilla in England in 1913 when he went out to establish the mission work in the Belgian Congo. Priscilla worked in the London headquarters and only saw her husband once in the last thirteen years of her life – that during a two-week visit she made to the Belgian Congo. The Harrisons' son, John, was raised to adulthood in England by his grandmother and only saw his father once after the age of three.

Ivor Davies in 1932 before he went to the Belgian Congo.

On the boat to the Belgian Congo, 1932 – Ivor Davies, back;
front from left, Daisy Kingdon, Irene James and Rosalie Sore.

Ivor and Rose, on their engagement in the Belgian Congo in 1933.

Ivor and Rose on their wedding day in Arua, Uganda, 13 September 1935.

The two couples, Ivor and Rose Davies and May and Vernon Willson, returning to the Congo in September 1935 after their weddings in Uganda.

The Davies family group in 1948, shortly before Ivor and Rose returned from
furlough to the Congo with the youngest children, Megan and Ruth, leaving the eldest, Ioan, Miriam and Evan at school in Scotland.

Ivor and Rose at the wedding of their daughter
Ruth to Maurice Charman. December 1972

Ivor Davies in 1954, about the
time of the Congo revival.

Rose and Ivor in the 1960s in New Zealand.

16

Changes in the Wind

Rose and Ivor returned in 1948 to a Belgian Congo that had subtly altered since they left in 1945, three years earlier. World War II produced tremendous changes in much of the world, and even in the isolated depths of the Ituri Forest. Congolese men conscripted to fight in the army brought back with them a new outlook on life, not always beneficial to village life. For example, incidences of theft in the villages noticeably increased. People who in the past had not moved more than a few hundred kilometres from their home for their entire lives now visualized another world not far away, especially in the cities where opportunities and money beckoned.

In addition to the new sense of materialism the government encouraged the indigenous population to produce more cotton, rice and peanuts in their village gardens. The traditional communal way of life of sharing what they owned began to breakdown as the people desired material possessions, often trying to outdo each other. After an initial dislike for cotton because they could not eat it, they found they could earn money for it at the markets. Soon each family had a cotton garden, enabling them to purchase bicycles, clothes, cloth and sewing machines.

Young people migrated to the cities in search of a better income, leaving behind their home gardens. That alarmed the government to such an extent that it began to restrict the movement of the indigenous population in order to keep the village gardens in production. Government officials asked local chiefs for the names of those who had left their locality. Then they tracked them down and forced them to return. The government's oppressive attitude, in that and in other situations, served to fan the flames of nationalism. The Opienge missionaries witnessed entire villages near the Angumu mines forced by a government whim to move from their existing location to another. The full backlash of the government's high-handed approach to the indigenous people would be harshly felt fifteen years later.

Some changes, however, were beneficial. Increased mobility resulted in the breaking down of negative tribal customs, such as the betrothal at birth of baby girls, the practice effectively enslaving Congolese women for countless generations.

Initially unaware of the changes the Davies were glad to return, for that was where the Lord had appointed them. They sailed to Mombasa by boat before travelling overland to the Congo. Their road journey was marked by several accidents, typical of travel in Africa. On the notorious Stanleyville Road their driver, Frank Cripps, steered too close to the side of the road and before they knew it they were all trapped in an upturned vehicle, shaken, but uninjured and able to clamber out.

The arduous fourteen-hour journey from Ibambi to Opienge included four large rivers, each involving slow and tedious crossings by barge. It had been raining heavily and the road become a quagmire, their car hopelessly bogged in the mud. Jack Scholes, the field leader, happened to be travelling the same road in the missionary truck and came to their rescue.

The final misadventure took place as Frank overtook a lorry slowly lumbering up a hill. The edge of the road was dangerously soft in the heavy rain and it collapsed, slewing the vehicle off the road and down a bank where it came to rest on its side. Thirty or forty villagers materialised for another rescue, helping them right it and push it back on the road.

The tumultuous African welcome in Opienge, worth the traumatic journey, lived up to their expectation, with the people crowding around the two returning missionaries and their children, faces beaming and shouting loudly in Congo-Swahili. They soon eased back into the busy daily routine, Ivor attending to his pastoral work, the construction around the station, boys' school and the adult literacy work. Rose re-established her medical work, attended to her pastoral duties with the women, oversaw the housework and cared for the girls.

Megan aged five and Ruth aged two adapted quickly to their new surroundings, becoming the centre of attention, with a crowd of local children congregating to watch them. By the end of the year both girls conversed freely in Congo-Swahili and played happily with the children of the indigenous Christians who worked and lived on the station. The bulk of the Davies' luggage did not turn up for months after their arrival, both Megan and Ruth rapidly outgrowing their clothing.

Not long after they returned Ivor and Rose lost their chief elder and friend of sixteen years. Ombengue was bitten by a snake and died from shock. He gave a remarkable testimony, stating he was ready to go and had nothing to fear. That made a great impression on the local people. Pagan deaths were often very different affairs, with fighting, screaming, people writhing on the ground and accusations as to who was responsible for the curse that killed the deceased. By contrast, Ombengue's funeral was peaceful and God-honouring.

Life, though hectic, was never dull. The Congolese were a fun-loving, demonstrative people who, despite all their problems, could dance and sing at times as if they had not a care in the world. There was always something new to see or a fresh problem to resolve. The missionaries were more than pastors, teachers, and nurses, for the Africans came to them to resolve their disputes and for advice on every conceivable matter. Ivor and Rose became as a father and mother to them, their advice highly respected.

They wrote regularly to their children in Scotland, advising and encouraging them as much as possible. Ioan, Miriam and Evan achieved well at school and spent enjoyable summer holidays with Ivor's family in Gowerton, Wales. Miriam startled them when she wrote about her plans to leave school once she was fifteen. Ivor and Rose both strongly encouraged her to stay and receive the sort of education they themselves had been denied in their youth.

The locals living on the station were interested in the progress of the three children in Britain. Snapshots sent to Ivor and Rose of the trio attracted a crowd who expressed amazement at the speed at which the children were growing. They enquired when they were going to visit and why they did not come in their school holidays. Despite Ivor's explanations concerning the distance to be travelled and the expense involved few comprehended the difficulties.

Near the end of 1948 Ivor started building a brick kiln, with the intention of firing bricks for rebuilding the bamboo and mud schoolhouse, the hostels and other station buildings in more permanent materials. Ivor made improvements to the sun-dried brick house he had built before furlough into which they moved on their return. During Christmas 1948 they conducted their regional Christian conference, held before the people became preoccupied picking their cotton harvest in early January.

But disaster struck in April 1949, with a momentous storm that brought high winds and heavy rain, blowing down seven buildings and badly damaging others. Ivor had 18,000 bricks ready for burning, to be used for the new school, all of which were destroyed, setting the work back months. Part of the leaf roof disappeared from the Davies' home and the girls' beds were saturated with the rain. Repair work was an ongoing reality of station life.

By 1949 the station's gardens had to feed 50 adults and a similar number of school children, requiring a considerable effort in food production. They yielded up to two tonnes of peanuts each year, harvested in June and July. Rose stored most of the crop to supplement the diet of the school children for the next twelve months and used the rest to make peanut butter. Any excess was sold at the markets to boost the church's funds to pay the evangelists' wages.

They planted rice as the rainy season began, normally in March, and it was harvested in late October in time for the markets in November. As well, they grew plantains, avocado, mango and orange trees. The fifteen orange trees planted around the station were prolific, producing far more than the station's population could consume, with the excess sold for church funds.

The same year, Opienge became an official Poste of the Belgian Congo Government, which built a large house 500 meters down the road to accommodate a Belgian official, his family, and his retinue which included Congolese soldiers. When Ivor and Rose arrived fourteen years earlier no Europeans lived in the area until Greek traders and their businesses arrived. The official and his wife proved to be congenial neighbours and regularly visited Ivor and Rose. The official's part-African daughter, Bernadette, spent hours playing with Megan and Ruth. The sisters were also delighted with the gift of two Siamese cats from a Angumu mine official.

Rose gave medical assistance to the wives of officials and Greek traders. Even in 1949 the nearest doctor was more than 200 kilometres away. She was happy to assist anyone, Congolese or otherwise, who came to her, but lamented the difficulty of obtaining medical supplies. She wished she had a pharmacy nearby or a Woolworths around the corner, such as she had in Wales, where she could buy medications or household goods. The mission did not provide money for schooling or medical work, nor for the care of the orphan children, so they prayed in the funds, trusting the Lord.

Rose did not keep records of the number of motherless children in her care before they left for furlough in 1945, but she began to keep an account after returning in 1948. By 1951 they were caring for six motherless children whom they had acquired in the four years, in addition to other older children they had taken in prior to their furlough. Rose continued to insist that a relative came to care for each child and she kept a careful eye on the caregivers to ensure the food was prepared correctly and meals were not overlooked. Tragic consequences had resulted through the ignorance of caregivers, with young babies dying because they were accidentally fed rubber plant sap, which resembled mother's milk.

New government regulations placed Rose in a tough position. An edict had been issued stating that all nurses in the Congo without diplomas were to cease treating patients. Although Rose had in the early 1930s completed fifteen months midwifery training and ten months general training in Britain, she had not gained a state registered nurse qualification. On the other hand, she had accumulated many years of practical experience, treating thousands of women in trying circumstances. The last baby born on the mission compound was named Onesimus, one of many toddlers later walking around with a biblical name.

Apart from Rose the only other person in the Opienge area with medical skills was a male Congolese nurse who ran a Government-sponsored dispensary a kilometre down the road from the station. There was a pressing need for women nurses with diplomas on stations like Opienge, remote from a doctor. With the government curtailing the work of nurses without diplomas health care and maternity oversight for women and girls were severely limited. Men could get help at dispensaries but Rose felt it was wrong to expose the Christian girls and women to the temptations and indignities of state dispensaries which knew nothing about midwifery and provided little or no nursing care for babies and children.

The locals failed to understand Rose's new reluctance to help them, for she had always assisted them in the past and they had confidence in her simple remedies. Though she knew little about modern drugs she did her best with love and prayer, undoubtedly saving many lives. But it was a strain to be responsible for the women in her orbit, with no doctor within calling distance.

Although she could not have a clinic on the station because she lacked the Bruxelles diploma she did not refuse any call to travel beyond and help where she could. Many were the times when she prayed in desperation about a difficult case and God answered her prayer. Since she had five children herself the women had confidence in her. In the long hours of waiting for the delivery of a baby she had the opportunity to get to know them, their troubles and customs – which she would not have had otherwise. It was a privilege to point them to the Lord.

Educating their two youngest children was demanding, with so much to distract them from their schoolwork. Ruth so enjoyed her African home that she often firmly declared that she did not want to go back to England "for a very long time." On occasions Ivor took either Megan or Ruth with him on a trek to the surrounding villages, his assistants transporting them in a sedan chair. By the age of nine Megan was sufficiently fluent in Congo-Swahili that she trekked with a new missionary, Sarah Ross, helping her to communicate with the villagers.

Rose stopped accompanying Ivor, unable to walk a great distance due to difficulties with her legs. The problem became so severe she was confined to the mission compound and forced to rest during the day, something she was loathe to do with her heavy work load. At first Rose was diagnosed with varicose veins, but after more than a year of suffering and seeking medical attention a doctor at Arua correctly diagnosed her problem as a double thrombosis. He immediately admitted her to Stanleyville Hospital, stating it was a miracle she was still alive, given the fact that she had not received the required rest or medical attention.

In 1949 David, Ivor's brother, married Anne Merritt, another HAM missionary who had arrived in 1943, further increasing the size of the extended family in the Congo. The couple travelled to Birmingham, England, to be married, and soon after returned to Africa. After six months at Poko they moved to Wamba to work as station leaders.

Ivor and Rose continued to notice changes in society and culture since their return in 1948. But there were also changes in the church and in the Christians themselves, especially in their attitudes. The former zeal was no longer there.

As the local pastors were not well paid, particularly in the poor Opienge region, many understandably supplemented their income with a garden. They soon forgot their priorities, spending most of their time gardening rather than working as effective pastors. In earlier times there would be a queue of evangelists outside the Davies' home at 6.00 a.m. each day, waiting for instructions regarding their area of work. By the late 1940s there was a pervasive atmosphere of apathy, the evangelists seeming to have lost their passion for winning others to the Lord. Ivor became increasingly disappointed with their lack of commitment.

The church was also plagued by a subtle increase in friction between Christians, the disharmony affecting both whites and blacks. Small differences developed into big issues. Good fellowship between fellow missionaries degenerated and gradually disappeared, causing real pain. Even in their own home the Davies experienced problems. Their houseboy[1] Davidi became so difficult that in November 1952 they considered dismissing him. He came and confessed small wrongs, but his critical spirit grew worse, as well as his laziness.

Apathy among the African Christians grew to a point where Ivor and Rose wondered whether it was time to move on. They became tired in their spirits with what appeared to be a losing battle and they felt like retreating in defeat. Outwardly the work made progress with the indigenous church increasing in size. Nevertheless, Ivor and

Rose were hungry to see growth in maturity, with individual lives reflecting real spiritual development.

The Opienge missionaries were not the only ones dissatisfied, for a similar attitude prevailed throughout the mission work. Sensing something was amiss, Jack Scholes, responsible for about 50 missionaries, visited all the stations to listen to concerns and to hear problems first-hand. On his return to the headquarters in Ibambi he sent out a written proposal, suggesting they set aside one day a month to pray and fast and seek the Lord to renew their vision and to experience revival.

The proposal was widely accepted and earnest prayer and fasting began. They longed for a new outpouring of God's Spirit to bring hope and new life. But nothing could have prepared either the missionaries or the African Christians for the incredible events which they were about to experience. They prayed for revival, but when it came it was not like anything they expected.

---

[1] To be a 'houseboy' was considered a privilege. Such a position should not be disparaged today as part of the colonial system. The government required foreigners to employ local people as a condition of their right to live there, and missionaries certainly needed help so they could fulfil their busy work load.

17

Have Your Way, Lord

On the third Thursday of the month the station was strangely quiet, in contrast to the usual tumult of activity centred on Ivor and Rose – teaching in the boys' school, overseeing maintenance work, home-schooling their two children, supervising workers in the Davies' home and gardens or attending to requests for minor medical assistance.

The locals wondered why the normal activities had come to a standstill, and why the missionaries did not have meals. The reason, they learned, was to seek the Lord and to renew their devotion to him. Workers joined them, and soon Christians in the surrounding villages prayed as well.

Ivor told them about the Rwanda Blessing, with the expectation that they might experience similar events themselves. In 1935 revival had broken out in countries to the east of the Congo, including Rwanda, Burundi and Uganda. Though mainly in Anglican areas it spread to other church affiliations, with its influence also felt in the church in the Congo.

Missionaries visiting Rwanda from the Congo observed a new quality of fellowship among the Christians, with barriers between Europeans and Africans broken. Meetings were marked by times of deep repentance and earnest prayer, followed by tremendous praise to the Lord, great joy, and many unbelievers becoming Christians.[1]

At the same time, some areas in the Congo also experienced a touch of spiritual renewal and revival. Sibling missionaries Jack, Lily and Ivy Roberts felt the lack of fervour in the church and prayed that God would move among them. Their prayers were answered with widespread repentance.[2] In 1949 there was another breeze of revival in both the Congo and in Rwanda.

Ivor also spoke of events in Korea.[3] American missionaries brought the gospel to Korea in the late ninteenth century, and when Korea became a Japanese protectorate in 1905, and was later annexed by Japan in 1910, the Korean church began to pray earnestly for their country in its time of humiliation. By 1906 revival came, with its huge prayer meetings, widespread repentance and many conversions.[4]

The Opienge missionaries prayed for a similar work of the Holy Spirit among themselves, though they were unaware as to what form that would take. The local Christians, too, longed for a deeper work in their hearts and for others to be saved.

After a few months intriguing things began to happen, although not until later did they realise their significance. The first unusual occurrence took place in May 1952, involving Alieni Paulo, an Opienge evangelist, who had words with his wife, Safiana, who could be a very irritating person. During the argument he picked up a small stick and struck her once on the arm. Immediately he was overcome with remorse, and cried out to the Lord all night to save him and wipe away his sin. He could not be comforted and his people were perplexed as to what to do. They called Esme Roupell who asked everyone to pray, and subsequently Aliene Paulo calmed down.

Some months later, in a village near Opienge a group of six pastors gathered for a six o'clock early morning prayer meeting as part of special gatherings convened for churches along the Angumu Road. Two hours later one of them asked the group to stop. He said he could not continue; he felt such a hypocrite because he knew he had problems with one of his Christian brothers. He confessed he was full of jealousy at the way his brother preached so powerfully and achieved results. The man's honesty immediately resulted in others confessing unforgiveness and hidden bitterness. Over the ensuing days, as they confessed and forgave each other, they sensed a greater love and closeness to one another and to God.

Ivor received a letter outlining the events which he shared with his missionary colleagues. They were pleased the Lord was prompting people to set their relationships right. But soon they had to face the truth that God wanted to work in their own lives, revealing their individual apathy, pride, disillusionment and lack of transparency. Before long they acknowledged that their joy had disappeared, praying together had become difficult and friction among them had increased. They had been expecting the Lord to work according to their preconceived plan for revival, but had been unaware that the Lord wished to move among themselves as well as the indigenous people.

God's dealings with Aliene Paulo and the six village pastors were but a foretaste of things to come, one of the most dramatic outpourings of God's Spirit ever recorded.

In February 1953, revival came first to the mission station of Lubutu, with the visit of the mysterious stranger[5] preaching a message of sin and repentance in a nearby village. In response, missionaries arranged a series of teaching sessions about the Holy Spirit and during that time a group of pastors cried out to receive him. God answered, sending the fires of anointing, along with repentance, confession and renewed spiritual life. The missionaries were astonished, at a loss as to how to respond. They had prayed for revival but what God sent was at first beyond their capacity to accept.

By May revival spread to Opienge. Ivor was absent, on a teaching circuit with Aubrey when he received a letter from Rose, describing recent events at the station.[6] She wrote about Sena who walked 200 kilometres to ask for forgiveness, and about Peleza who surprised everyone with her loud nocturnal worship of the Lord. She then shared the vision Peleza received, with the message of cleaning away the ashes before lighting God's fire. Finally she told of Peleza's noisy worship during the Sunday service when Sarah was attempting to preach.

Ivor read and reread the letter, the knot of fear and apprehension growing in his stomach. He did not understand. Were the events the work of God or of Satan? He knew that on his return to Opienge people would inundate him, as the station leader, with questions. He was frightened because of his inability to provide the answers.

"Lord, what is this all about? What am I going to do?" he pleaded.

It was then that he had a completely new experience. To his amazement he saw a graphic vision. On the rough wall of the living room there was his own mission station with people crowding into the meeting hall. To his shock he watched the same things happening as had been described by the Lubutu missionaries at their station. Some people were raising up their arms loudly rejoicing, some were falling over the seats, while others were on the floor screaming in pain. He stared and stared at the vision before he turned away and hid his face in his hands, longing for the images to go away. Silently he questioned the Lord as to what it was about.

He looked at the wall again to see if the vision was still there. The first picture had disappeared but there was another in its place – an upright rock, with red blood flowing across it, which then congealed. The picture disappeared. Ivor looked at Aubrey, who was still sitting in the corner of the room reading his letter, obviously unaware of the visions or Ivor's troubled thoughts. He gathered up his letter and went into the bedroom, flinging himself down by the bed.

"Lord, what is happening?" he cried. "I haven't experienced visions like these before. What about those people I saw in the church?

What does the vision mean?"

Straight away he heard the Lord speak to his heart, "You're afraid of what people will say. You're not willing for me to have my way." Ivor knew it was true. He did not want to write home and tell people what was happening. He did not want them to conclude the missionaries were straying from the orthodox path and tolerating strange occurrences.

"It's true, it's fear of man," he said, "and Lord, I don't want this fear to grip and control me. I want you to have your way."

Again he sensed the Lord say, "Do you really want me to have my way?"

"Yes, Lord," Ivor replied, and peace flowed into his heart.

He considered again the second vision, the rock with the congealed blood on it. He had no idea of its meaning. He asked the Lord and waited for an answer, but nothing came.

The next day Ivor was still fearful about the visions and he longed to run from the situation he knew he would have to face at Opienge. He did not feel free to tell his younger companion, Aubrey, of his inner struggles. After all, how would Aubrey respond to Ivor's claims that he had just experienced strange visions? They had known each other only a few months. Perhaps Aubrey would think that malaria, or Ivor's many years under the African sun, had finally taken toll on his mind.

Having completed their planned circuit of the villages Ivor and Aubrey rode their bicycles back to Opienge. While Ivor still felt anxious about the recent developments he was wary of offending the Lord by harbouring a wrong attitude. The following day Peleza spoke to him about her experiences, wanting to set the record straight as there were rumours that she had gone insane.

Later that day Ivor sat on his verandah trying without success to write a sermon. He could not get away from the vision of the rock covered with congealed blood. It bothered him that he did not understand its meaning or significance. He put down his Bible.

"Lord, what's it all about?" he longed to know.

Feeling prompted to consult a dictionary he discovered that the word 'congealed' was a process that happened to some liquids when they met a cold surface.

Suddenly he realised the Lord was talking about his own heart towards God. The Lord wanted his blood to flow and people to be cleansed. The first vision spoke about his fear of people and the second indicated that his heart was hard and cold, preventing him from letting God have his way.

Ivor broke down and sobbed.

"Lord, I'm not holding back anymore," he wept. "I came out to Africa to preach about the cleansing power of your blood and I don't want anything to stop that. Have your way, Lord."

[1] Norman Grubb, *Mighty through God*, pages 97-99.

[2] Evan Davies, *Whatever happened to CT Studd's mission?* Page 45.

[3] Colin Whittaker, *Great Revivals*, pages 138-41.

[4] In both Rwanda and Korea times of revival were followed by great suffering and persecution, which seems to be a divine pattern for some areas. The Democratic Republic of the Congo was to follow a similar path. Korea today is reaping the benefits of revival with its huge churches, packed early-morning prayer meetings and programmes for sending out missionaries.

[5] See chapter 1.

[6] Esme Roupell moved to another station earlier in 1953.

18

Asenti, Asenti, Bwana Yesu

The visions of Peleza and Ivor both pointed to the same thing – the ashes in the fireplace and the blood on the rock demonstrated that God was preparing to clean out people's hearts. And Ivor, as station leader, was to be one of the first.

Over the next few days in May 1953, Ivor knew he was directly under the Lord's spotlight. God spoke to him about his relationship with Rose. They loved each other and had both come to Africa to serve as missionaries. But there were times when Ivor was impatient or demanding. He would come indoors from the hot African sun and, if things were not right or dinner was late, he would snap at her. At other times, when the whole family was inside with the children playing on the floor and making a noise, he would find it difficult to concentrate on his message preparation. He would then reprimand Rose for not keeping 'her' children quiet.

"Aren't they your children as well?" he felt the Lord say. "Do you think such comments are kind?" Ivor knew they were not, and he asked Rose for her forgiveness. There were other things as well that he sorted out with her, assuming God was finished with him. But, no, not at all.

"What about the missionary in charge of the girls' school?" the Lord questioned him. "What has happened in the last few months? You've been unwilling for her to conduct the girls' services as usual and there's been friction between you. Both of you sit at the same meal table and you're very polite to her, but there is something wrong. Go to her and put it right."

Ivor reasoned that he was the station leader and she should come to him to sort out their lack of accord. But the Lord pointed to Ivor's pride, which was unacceptable. So Ivor approached her.

The Lord moved to his relationship with the Africans, in particular a worker whom Ivor had taught building skills and given work. When he did things contrary to Ivor's expectations he chided him in a hurtful manner. In the pulpit he was the minister preaching love, but in the workshop he showed a different face. Also in the boys' school he had taken harsh action against several of the students and hurt them, for which he needed to apologise.

"Me, a teacher, apologising to a boy!" Ivor objected with vigour. That was a costly step, but after he went to see them peace filled his heart and mind.

There were more issues. He remembered comments in his correspondence in circular letters to Britain. He had to write and present the correct picture. Another time he was sitting in his study looking up at the book shelf on the wall when he realised several were not his. He sent them back to their owners with a word of apology. Then there was an apparently trivial matter. When he was at Bible college another student departed, leaving behind a pair of pliers. Ivor thought he did not want them so he put them in his kit and later took them to the Congo. The Lord pointed out that they were not his. They had been left at the Bible college, so they belonged to the college and he was to send them back. Ivor posted them to Wales with a letter apologizing for his actions.

There came a time when Ivor thought there could not possibly be anything else for the Lord to deal with.

"Yes, there is one more thing," the Lord said. "I want you to tell the people about my dealings with you."

Ivor was horrified. "No Lord, I can't do that. I've been here eighteen years, I have married many of the people. I've dedicated their children. I've counselled them and they're like my children. I can't stand up in front of them and tell them these things. I just can't do it!"

"Yes, you will," he said. "No blessing until you do."

Soon after, he conducted the normal Sunday meeting. They sang more choruses than usual and Ivor knew he could procrastinate no longer. He had to tell them his journey. As he spoke the blessing and anointing of the Holy Spirit fell on him in an impressive and powerful way. The gathered congregation had not seen him with the same authority and anointing before and they came up to him afterwards to express their amazement and admiration.

The service ushered in a series of memorable and momentous days. On Thursday the Christians gathered for their regular monthly day of prayer and fasting. Peleza had spoken to Ivor the evening before, asking for the men's and women's prayer meetings to be held separately, as she wanted to speak to the women by themselves. The women's meeting began at 7.00 a.m. and continued to 10.00 a.m. Peleza told the women what God had instructed her to say.

"Anyone with a bag of sin hidden away in your hearts is to open it up and make confession, so that God can do a great work in you." The message resulted in many women confessing their sins to each other.

The men's meeting began at about 9.30 am and, after Ivor encouraged them to be open to the Holy Spirit, the men began to pray. Evangelist Alieni Paulo rose to his feet, a different tone in his prayer, one of earnest pleading. As he prayed he grew agitated and began crying, his tears flowing freely, and then he collapsed into his seat. For a few moments there was silence. Then chief elder Matalembo, Peleza's husband, a very tall man, shot up to his full height, his hands stretched out, shaking and shouting at the top of his voice,

"Asenti, asenti, asenti, asenti, Bwana Yesu, Hallelujah! Thank you, thank you."

The whole place became charged as if with an electric current. Everywhere men were falling, jumping, laughing, crying, shouting, singing, confessing or shaking violently. It was an extraordinary sight. Some confessed their sin at length, like elder Alili, who cried in repentance for three quarters of an hour, while others, with nothing to confess, raised their voices in praise. One man came on his hands and knees from the back of the room right up to the front, expressing his reverence to the Lord. Benoit, a young evangelist, was filled with the Spirit, shaking and jumping all over the place. Then he quietened down and began praising the Lord in a wonderful manner such as the missionaries had not heard before, his praises seeming to ascend all the way up to the throne of God, with joy unbounded.

Meanwhile, the women came out of their meeting and gathered around the windows to see the awe-inspiring spectacle of their men caught up with the Lord. Instead of going to their homes to prepare food for their families they returned to their meeting place. Hardly had they gone inside when the Spirit came on them, with the same manifestations as the men experienced. All Ivor and the other missionaries could say was, "Amazing! Just amazing!" The two meetings continued until about 1.00 pm, but even after they left the meeting places people were seen falling down, praising the Lord, or confessing their sins on the paths or in the villages.

The afternoon meeting was a combined one. What a gathering it was – like a turbulent spiritual tornado where people were literally flung to the floor over seats, yet not one was injured. Ivor had been reading *The Rent Heavens* by R.B. Jones, a book about the Welsh Revival. It made mention of an evangelist who could hardly make his voice heard above the din of worshipping saints. Ivor's spirit leapt for joy, knowing they in the Congo were experiencing the same anointing of the Holy Spirit.

During the meeting Ivor felt he should challenge the occasional excess of emotionalism. Several women who were flung to the floor, rolled over and over, taking no account of their clothing. As they generally wore only a wrap around themselves they were soon undressed and Ivor had to intervene. He spoke of the Holy Spirit being, by his very nature, holy, never countenancing indecency of any sort. The people responded well to his exhortation and teaching, accepting his words backed by scripture without question.

Girls from the school were present, as well as two or three schoolboys, and the Lord touched and blessed them. One of them, Mateo, was filled by the Spirit in the morning meeting, and became very involved in the afternoon worship. It was his turn to draw the Davies' water for the month. Two or three times during the following days he was thrown to the floor of their cookhouse, shouting praises to the Lord and urging others to get right with the Lord.

That evening the missionaries gathered for prayer and discussion about the events of the day. None of them had ever seen anything like it before and they still wondered if it was of the Lord or not. Though there were a great many things they did not understand they felt the Lord blessed them with unity between themselves. Ivor had attended numerous inspiring prayer meetings at the Bible College of Wales in Swansea, when the Spirit anointed everyone in power, but he had experienced nothing like the events of that day. He suggested they prayed for the gift of the spirit of discernment, something he later believed the Lord answered.

They felt the special happenings were in line with Acts 2, where the prophet Joel spoke of God pouring out his Spirit on all people. Their sons and daughters would prophesy, their young men would see visions, their old men would dream dreams, and on their servants, both men and women, God would pour out his Spirit. During their evening prayers they had been reading through Jeremiah, having progressed as far as chapter 31. They were particularly encouraged by verse 34 which spoke of all knowing the Lord who would 'forgive their iniquity and remember their sin no more'.

The next day, Friday, was a humbling experience for the missionaries, for they had to listen to confession after confession of the things that the people held against them. Many came to ask them for forgiveness for the many times they had murmured or grumbled against them. Ivor questioned in his heart the reality of some of the confessions, challenging those who confessed to stealing to make restitution. He found their ready response pleasing.

On Saturday, a conference began. It was one of two local conferences held each year at Opienge, with up to a thousand people attending from the surrounding villages, some walking 160 kilometres for the ten days of teaching, prayer and fellowship. Thus it was a prearranged event, but in retrospect dovetailed neatly with the rising momentum of revival.

Ivor was most anxious. Despite all he had seen and the way God had allayed many of his fears he held concerns for the gathering. It was one thing for the Holy Spirit to fall on a small meeting of those living on the station. But what would happen if the Spirit descended during a large conference gathering? It did not bear thinking about.

Preparations had been underway for weeks prior, with the station families organising food and gathering huge amounts of firewood. Extra plantain, the ubiquitous staple diet of the region, was brought in from other areas, as the station gardens were unable to supply sufficient for such a large gathering.

Groups of Christians arrived, singing hymns and waving palm fronds. The first sound of hymn-singing in the distance was the signal for the station's Congolese residents, school children and adults, to run to greet the new arrivals and escort them in. Before seeking accommodation the visitors crowded around the missionaries, offering 'salaams' and handshakes. Where the large numbers slept was always a mystery, for every available space was used.

On Saturday evening Ivor held the first meeting for the new arrivals. The 400 who gathered were mainly men and older children, for most of the women were bedding down their infants. Ivor hoped for a subdued beginning to the conference, so he decided beforehand to give a word of welcome, urge the people to be ready for the Lord to work in their hearts, briefly tell them about the previous Thursday, say a short prayer and immediately send the visitors to their sleeping quarters.

"I realise you are tired tonight," Ivor told his audience, "so there will be no message and you can all get to sleep early. Let us pray . . ." Ivor had no sooner opened his mouth to start praying when the Holy Spirit fell on the congregation. He was stunned. What he had seen in his first vision out in the village he now witnessed in reality. He trembled with the power of the Holy Spirit.

"Stop! Stop!" Ivor cried, but to no avail. He prayed a benediction but nobody left the building. He turned to Aubrey sitting behind him. Aubrey shrugged his shoulders and raised his eyebrows as if to say, "Don't look at me. I don't know what to do!" All Ivor could do was stand and watch what was taking place before him. He found the screaming and shouting completely unnerving. People were falling down, even women with children in their arms. Ivor was grateful no one was injured. Rose heard the commotion from their house where she was looking after the two children, likening it to the roar of a large waterfall descending many metres.

Inside the meeting the missionaries witnessed an astonishing and incredible sight. People were filled with the power and presence of the Lord, literally drunk with the Spirit. Never, never had they seen anything like it. Elders and evangelists were swept to their feet, reeling around like drunken men, shouting, "I am filled, I am filled". Some turned to Ivor and ask for forgiveness for having criticised him. As soon as he said he forgave them they praised the Lord with real joy and great shouts.

They went to one another, or called out a name at the other end of the church, asking for forgiveness for a wrong done. Some called out the name of their wife, telling her he was filled with the Spirit and asking her not to hold out against the Lord. Some described the experience of receiving 'the blessing' like a shower coming upon them. Then their hearts fluttered like birds and prayer poured from their mouths.

Aliasi, an evangelist, began to weep and Ivor asked him what was wrong. He confessed that he had been making wrong entries in his report book, where he recorded the villages he had visited, and he begged Ivor to forgive him. As soon as he said he would Aliasi began to shout praises to the Lord. He then made a public confession of his wrong report book entries. The meeting continued with a joy that seemed to know no limits.

Finally Ivor felt led to clap his hands and begin singing *Onward Christian Soldiers* in Congo-Swahili. Immediately the whole congregation as one stood on their feet. Ivor later wrote, "Was there ever any singing like it? No, not even in my native Wales, except perhaps during the 1904 Revival."

On and on the singing went, every line and verse with punctuated emphasis, people glancing at their neighbour with a smile and a nod of the head, indicating their fullness of joy at the victory of Jesus over the Enemy. The last verse was one of praise, first to the Father, then to the Son, and to the Holy Spirit. There was such a volume of praise that Ivor wondered if angels stopped their ministering to gaze down at the wonderful sight. They repeated the hymn again and again, until "Hallelujah" and "Praise the Lord" ended the wonderful meeting and they drifted out of the building about midnight. For many there was no sleep, but singing, praising and seeking the Lord all through the night.

Before retiring, the five missionaries prayed together for wisdom and understanding. Ivor had been asleep in bed a while when he thought

Rose was trying to wake him. It felt as though she had thrown her arm on his chest. When he looked across the bed he realised she was fast asleep. But he was convinced he felt an arm on his chest. Then he understood the Lord had woken him. He asked him why he tried to stop the people when the Holy Spirit first fell in the meeting. Ivor recognised he was still fearful. He believed everything in church ought to be done with 'decency and order'. The Lord showed him sin was the cause of confusion, not himself. As soon as sin was confessed peace and order resulted. Ivor understood and he fell asleep.

19

A Momentous Conference

Sunday, the first full day of the conference, was extraordinary. There was little need to summon everyone to the church service. Long before the prayer drum sounded the building was packed beyond its comfortable capacity with eager and expectant people. Word had already reached the villages concerning the previous night's events, and even non-Christians arrived to peer inside to see with their own eyes that which they had been told. Ivor squeezed his way to the pulpit through the throng of people and started a chorus.

The spiritual tempo grew, along with faith and expectancy. Ivor knew it would be difficult to preach a message so he thought he should use the meeting to encourage people individually to get right with the Lord. Some of the pastors stood at his side. Ivor caught the eye of one of them and knew immediately from his expression that he had similar thoughts. So they moved among the people, urging them to repent and confess their sin.

Ivor recognised that the Lord was working in different ways among the people. Some, in a healthy relationship with the Lord, were immediately filled with the Holy Spirit and with great joy. Others were convicted of sin, but were filled after they confessed and asked for the Lord's mercy, like the man lying on the floor pleading for forgiveness. He went to the government office later to confess his non-payment of taxes.

However, others were convicted of sin but not immediately filled with the Holy Spirit. Some, after asking for forgiveness, thought they were filled with the Spirit but there was no joy, unlike those who were immediately filled. At first they would shake violently, or appear to be overcome with great conviction of sin, or be thrown to the ground, and it seemed they were filled with the Spirit, but the realisation came to Ivor that it was not so.

He saw the danger of believing that they had received all, seeing they had an experience of shaking, strong conviction and forgiveness of sin. But, in fact, they had not received everything and there was more for them to discover. The leaders had to make sure they were really filled with the Holy Spirit, and not just an empty clean house, open for the Enemy to re-inhabit at a later time.

Ivor knew that some who still practised polygamy or other sins were only too pleased to falsely believe that they had the Holy Spirit, because they had been shaken beyond their control. They came to see that they had to put their houses in order and earnestly seek the fullness of the Spirit.

That Sunday the Lord led them to make use of 'prompters'. When someone came up the front to confess their sins, but did not seem to make a full confession, the Holy Spirit came down on others who urged them to bring all to the light, holding nothing back. A young man, Tomasi, and an old man, a gardener, both operated as prompters. They were ordinary people yet those confessing responded to their promptings for they were anointed by the Holy Spirit.

Some confessors were in such agony, under heavy conviction, with their crying heartbreaking. There was nothing Ivor could do except urge people to pray. The sincere attitude of prayer became a feature of the meetings. As soon as a person rose to pray the whole congregation prayed simultaneously, some standing, some sitting, with no disorder or confusion.

The days of the conference continued in a similar pattern. Throughout the entire event Ivor and his fellow missionaries witnessed dramatic activities of the Holy Spirit. At each meeting 40 or more people queued near the pulpit, eagerly waiting an opportunity to testify to God's dealings with them. The congregations heard confessions to everything from murder to petty theft, things the missionaries had not the slightest idea about, some of many years' standing. It was a deep thrill for them to see some as young as seven or eight years standing to share what God had done for them and pleading in prayer for others.

Ivor understood what he was witnessing paralleled the accounts he had heard and read regarding the 1904 Welsh Revival. Over the years he had given much thought as to why the Welsh Revival appeared not to have a long-lasting impact on his homeland. Many in Wales had personally experienced a tremendous outpouring of the Holy Spirit, yet it seemed their faith in God ebbed away when exposed to heretical teaching.

Ivor therefore looked for opportunities for teaching and exhortation from the Word. He knew it was said that ministers in past visitations did not do enough solid preaching and teaching, often prioritising testimonies and prayer. By continually teaching from the Bible, his people understood the truth and responded well. The quoting of scriptures became a prominent feature of their testimonies and prayers.

It was a demanding time for the missionaries as they cautiously set about discerning whether or not some manifestations were of God. While they wanted the work of the Holy Spirit to be uninhibited they did not want people to be led astray by counterfeit and deception. To that end they relied on what they knew to be right according to the Bible and on the discernment given to them by the Holy Spirit.

During the week of the conference Ivor tested the spirit of those who appeared to move under the Spirit's influence by asking them questions: Did they have a love for the truth, and were they sensitive to it? What was their attitude to a lie? Was it hateful to them? Were they willing, as far as it was possible, to put a wrong right, by making restitution and by being willing to confess and ask forgiveness of the person wronged? Were they willing to make a public confession of the Lord Jesus? Was the praise given to the Lord?

The test of making restitution proved to be significant over and over again as people made genuine efforts to make amends for their wrongdoings. They travelled long distances and wrote letters to clear up misunderstandings. In the meetings some cried as if their hearts were breaking because they had misrepresented something, and then they pleaded for forgiveness. Others audibly and sympathetically assented when a person was confessing, bringing out with deep emotion a long concealed wrong. On the other hand they were very sensitive if truth was violated and they protested with loud cries.

When the Spirit came upon Davidi, Ivor and Rose's houseboy, he stood and made a full confession about all that he had stolen from the family, and then he brought them money to pay for the needles and cash he had stolen. He said in his testimony that one of his daily tasks was to make the beds, while his 'white lady' was busy with her duties at the school or the medical clinic, but he did not do the job thoroughly. Since the Holy Spirit came into his life he made the beds properly every day.

He had also stolen kerosene from a trader but was afraid to confess it and repay him in case he was put in prison. When he was challenged with the example of Zacchaeus in the Bible he said he was ready, even if it meant prison. The same trader and his wife were amazed at the number of people who confessed similar thefts from them, and much prayer was made for the trader to come to the Lord.

As far as the question of praise to the Lord was concerned, there had never been such praise before in the area. Ivor previously thought that Congo Swahili, as a language, did not lend itself to the expression of wonderful praise, but afterwards realised the Holy Spirit knew the etymology of language inside out, and caused the people to praise the Lord from hearts full of joy, making it a beautiful thing. He was grateful for the privilege of being there to experience it.

During the week of special meetings they saw the enemy trying to lead people astray. The first time was in an evening meeting where some repeated their testimonies of confession, which they had given the previous night. When the Holy Spirit brought it to his attention Ivor challenged the next person about it. But the subsequent one to speak did exactly the same thing and Ivor recognised a spirit of unbelief at work in the young converts. He stopped the testimonies and asked the people to pray. After a time of earnest prayer they reached a place of knowing they had the victory. Everyone rose to their feet and sang triumphantly *Stand up, stand up for Jesus.*

The next night the enemy was at work again with a different method. A number of people were under deep conviction of sin, crying, pleading and trembling. However Ivor noticed that afterwards some of them sat down quietly without asking forgiveness. When the pattern was repeated Ivor challenged them, but found it very difficult to persuade them to ask for forgiveness. As on the previous night he asked the people to pray against the enemy in the name of the Lord and they had another battle in prayer until they had the assurance of victory.

After that the same tactics were not repeated, although there were other potential problems. For example, people attempted to work up an encounter with the Holy Spirit. Elder Alumeti saw his friends being blessed but he himself had no such experience. Aubrey and Ivor looked in his direction during one meeting and saw him glancing around at others who were obviously filled with the Spirit. Then they saw him trying to work up a blessing by shaking and trembling all over. After a few minutes he realised it was not working and he gave up, appearing very sorry for himself for the rest of the evening.

A few weeks later, at an outstation, Aubrey heard him testify, after he had experienced a real anointing, of his attempt to work up the blessing and his subsequent failure. His case, and that of others, gave them the opportunity to point out the dangers of counterfeit, a device the devil would use for his own ends.

Another case concerned a man who for years had wanted to be someone important. The elders had rebuked him time and time again for his sinful lifestyle. He came to Ivor early one morning saying the Spirit had given him a message as well as a hymn that did not make any sense. He was to come to Ivor, he said, and, with no one else present and behind closed doors he was to lay hands on him that he might receive the Spirit. Knowing the man and his desire to be thought of consequence by his tribe Ivor saw through his words and challenged him in the name of Jesus, questioning that he had ever received the Holy Spirit. The man went away and did not bother Ivor or the people any further.

Day after day the Holy Spirit continued to touch people. Many temporarily left the conference to return to their villages, seeking the forgiveness of their husbands or wives, their neighbours or chiefs, or to return things they had stolen. Some went to government officials to return picks and shovels they had stolen while serving prison sentences or undertaking road maintenance. It was a common belief among the Congolese that the government was sufficiently wealthy to sustain the loss of a few tools. The degree of such theft soon became apparent when officials were inundated with huge stacks of returned stolen tools.

One curious outcome of the revival was the sudden surge in tax payments or the making of amends for the non-payment of tax. Officials near Opienge came to Ivor because they had heard rumours of the unusual events that were taking place. When more people started paying taxes the officials understood what Ivor had said was true – the people had, without doubt, turned over a new leaf.

After the conference the confessions, the pleas for forgiveness, and the restitutions continued throughout the Opienge region. Shopkeepers heard confessions from people who had stolen items. Some of them even began to turn away confessing thieves because the shopkeepers themselves came under conviction for the wrong-doing they in turn had perpetrated in the past.

The missionaries praised the Lord that they and the evangelists and elders were in unity during those wonderful meetings. Together they prayed that everyone would remain strong and committed as they faced again the challenges of ordinary life.

20

Confessions, Restitution and Visions

After the conference, people returned to their villages and the mission station to its busy routine. There were 60 boys and 60 girls in residence at the schools, together with 50 prospective evangelists, the workmen and their wives. Everyone had something to put right or debts to settle. The Davies' former houseboy arrived with a new floral soup plate, wanting Rose to accept it because he had smashed so many dishes. At first they were inclined to refuse offers, but realised they should accept the restitution for the sake of the person's peace of mind. In cases of real hardship, where people were unable to make restitution, they forgave the offence and cancelled the debt.

They found God did not differentiate between so-called 'large' and 'small' sins and were surprised at the sensitivity of the Holy Spirit to what they termed the small ones. Breaking commandments regarding murder, adultery and theft were understood as real sins, but God was not so particular, people believed, about heart sins like murmuring, evil thoughts and criticism. When they came under conviction over such sins they saw them from God's viewpoint.

Tunziako, the wife of an elder, had spoken frequently against one of the missionaries and for days she struggled with the Spirit's conviction. She stood to confess her sin, trembling strongly, but she received no freedom or joy. Later, she began quaking again and crying pathetically, asking for a particular hymn to be sung. Still there was no freedom.

She became unable to walk and Ivor was asked to go see her. He took Aubrey with him and they found Tunziako sitting on a low stool, her legs incapable of moving. Ivor tried to help her rise but it was impossible. Her legs seemed stuck to the ground. They sat down near her, while she cried miserably, and then began to confess with great sorrow her sin of speaking against the missionary. As soon as she had finished she was filled with joy. Her knees straightened and she stood up and walked. It was one of the first cases of 'fixings' that were later to become commonplace for a period.

Church meetings on the station took on a new dimension after the dramatic outpouring of God's Spirit at the conference. The Congolese had a new vitality in their Christian walk and a passionate zeal to see others won to the Lord. Some meetings were so full of joy, prayer, and praise to God that Ivor was faced with a problem that pastors of Western countries would envy. The praise meetings went on hour after hour until Ivor had to ask the Lord to withhold his Spirit as they were not physically capable of giving praise anymore.

It had been the practice in meetings for one person at a time to stand and pray. Ivor now found it most disconcerting when, as soon as one person rose to their feet, ten or twenty others started praying simultaneously. The practice seemed contradictory to the Bible's instruction to do everything 'decently and in order', and Ivor tried to stop it. But the Lord spoke in his heart, "Trust Me, I'm in charge. There are people praying all over the world at the same time and I hear them all." It became a common occurrence for several to pray at the same time, or even the whole church together.

One of the local women received a vision along similar lines. She was told that united prayers did not arrive at the ears of God in confusion. Rather, the prayers united into one plea that was very acceptable to the Father. Not long after, Ivor felt God's prompting to listen closely to the multitude of prayers ascending in the meeting. It dawned on him that everyone was praying for the same man, Avuka, though no instruction had been given to do so. The man had been an elder eight year's prior but had backslidden. The congregation prayed earnestly for him and after twenty minutes, the prayer gave way to singing and praise.

The following Sunday Ivor tried to preach, with people calling out hymns to sing or starting to pray. He told them they must listen, for there had to be a place for the preaching of the Word of God. Then a man came up to him and said there was someone at the door to see him. Exasperated, Ivor said he could not because he was preaching. He was told it was Avuka, the man the church had prayed for the previous Thursday night. Though he lived 30 kilometres away he had come to church. Ivor invited him in and it transpired he wanted to speak to everyone, not just to Ivor.

Avuka told how he had gone to bed about 9.00 pm on Thursday night but could not sleep, his mind on the time when he was a church elder. A great longing came into his heart to be reconciled with the Lord. Finally he rose, made a fire, and sat warming himself beside it. His wife got up and asked him what was troubling him.

"I've longed for some time for you to return to the Lord," she said when he told her his thoughts.

"Get the book," he asked her, and he read a portion of the Bible. Then he prayed that the Lord would allow him to return to him, unaware the church was praying for him that very same night. The congregation was amazed when they heard his story and praised God for the answered prayer.

People received words of knowledge from the Lord. One man sitting at the front of a gathering got up and said that a woman who had just entered was not in right fellowship with the Lord. He turned around and repeated several times that she must seek the Lord's forgiveness. Finally she stood up at the back and admitted she was the person, for she had not had a time of prayer and Bible reading that morning.

"No, that's not it," the man countered. "Tell the people. Tell the people or else I will state what the Lord has revealed to me."

"I will tell you," the woman said as she shot to her feet again. Then she confessed she had been unfaithful to her husband. The man at the front was most relieved that he did not have to announce her sin to everyone.

Prayer became so important to the Opienge Christians that three extra evening prayer meetings were convened. They prayed that the blessing would spread to other stations, not just in the HAM work, but to other mission organisations.

People received visions, especially about the Second Coming. One of the reliable women described a vision she had of the rapture – of the Lord coming in the clouds and of hearing the trumpet of God, of lots of people on earth looking up, and of people leaving the ground, gently ascending to meet the Lord. Then she saw the people left behind, looks of horror on their faces, some spreading out their arms and trying to rise, but unable to do so. The congregation was very moved by her word.

God also worked in the Davies children. Ten-year-old Megan had been reading a book called *Taken or Left*, based on the Bible story of the two women in the field, one of whom was taken to heaven and the other left behind. One evening Megan called her mother from bed, saying she did not want to be left behind, but wanted Jesus to come to her and be in her. Rose encouraged her to get out of bed, kneel down and invite Jesus into her life.

A few nights' later, Lokiwa, a young schoolgirl, had a vision. She was in the Spirit in her bedroom, not asleep, when she saw a large beautiful place with many people arriving, dressed in white, like the Opienge school girls in their best clothes on Sunday. She saw

Ivor enter, followed by Rose and four of their five children. Then Lokiwa burst out crying.

"There was no little Ruth," she said, and she pleaded in prayer for the youngest child, Ruth. The following morning Ivor told the story at breakfast time, with eight- year old Ruth listening closely. That night, just as she went to bed, she called her mother, telling her that she, too, did not wish to be left behind and that she wanted to accept the Lord Jesus as her Saviour. She got out of bed and onto her knees, and gave her life to the Lord.

Dinner in the Davies' household was interrupted one evening by a man wailing loudly outside. Such crying usually indicated someone had died, so Ivor went out to investigate. As he stepped through the door the man, Etiene, fell at his feet.

"Get the book, get the book!" he yelled. Ivor had recently experienced similar cases where people, under conviction of sin, had run to him, wanting a specific passage read out.

Ivor retrieved his Bible from the house and took him to his office. Etiene requested Ivor read from 1 Corinthians 3: "Don't you know that you yourselves are God's temple and that God's Spirit lives in you? If anyone destroys God's temple, God will destroy him; for God's temple is sacred and you are that temple".

"It's me!" he screamed when Ivor read the word 'destroy', and he slumped again at Ivor's feet, clinging to his leg. He had been earlier sitting outside his house by the fire while Nuni, his wife, prepared the evening meal. Suddenly he began to jump around.

"I'm burning. It's raining hot fire. I'm burning," he yelled to his wife. She told him it was not raining but he continued to leap around, insisting he was being burnt by drops of hot rain. Finding no relief he ran to the mission station, first to the Browns' house, then to the Davies' home. Addressing him as a brother Ivor told him the Lord would not destroy him if he confessed whatever was wrong.

Etiene had come to Christ in the initial stages of the revival and was greatly blessed by the Lord. He confessed to Ivor he had gone to another station to tell the missionary there what had happened at Opienge. When she left the room, he saw her watch and pocketed it, taking it back to his village. It was not until he reached home, a distance of 320 kilometres, that the Lord convicted him of the sin. After confessing it to Ivor Etiene walked the long distance back to the station to return the watch and confess it to the missionary. He later became an evangelist.

One day Louis, the Browns' cook, failed to turn up for work, reporting he was ill. That evening he came running to Ivor's office in an agony of conviction, saying the Spirit had kept him home, unable to get his legs to function properly. The Spirit told him he was not physically sick and that he would not die, but he needed him to confess his sins. In great agony Louis took hold of Ivor's hands as if he had the strength of ten men and shouted out his sins at the top of his voice. Ivor asked him not to shout so loudly but he said the Spirit made him. When it was over and he had received assurance of forgiveness he beamed from ear to ear in great relief, praise pouring from his lips.

Congolese men who were sentenced to imprisonment, often unjustly for some minor infringement, sometimes used their incarceration to help themselves to hand tools used in the prison work. Five years earlier Ali had been imprisoned and on the last day of his prison term he was designated a job in a stone quarry. That evening he left the pick-axe and a machete among the rocks. A month later he returned to see if they were still there and when he found them he took them home. But the Lord convicted him and after a struggle against the fear of reimprisonment, he took them back. Government officials were astonished at the sudden honesty of the Congolese whom they categorised as 'liars and thieves'. They could not help wonder at the transformation that had taken place in so many lives.

Ivor was hesitant to report in detail to supporters in Britain what was taking place. What he and his fellow missionaries witnessed was well beyond the personal experiences of the vast majority of British Christians, apart from those who were alive during the Welsh Revival 50 years earlier. He feared they would think he had allowed the situation to get out of hand and they would withdraw their backing. Fortunately the HAM home committee in London was very excited and supportive and encouraged Ivor not to inhibit the work of the Holy Spirit.

Among the missionaries in the Congo there was a mixed reaction. While the field leader, Jack Scholes, and others were very encouraging some were astonished at Ivor's reports and others disapproved completely, putting events down to excessive emotionalism. On the other hand, some who welcomed the revival felt they would have experienced greater blessing if all the missionaries had been of one heart, with the negative attitudes of some grieving the Holy Spirit.

One of the first to receive a report from Ivor was his brother David and his wife Anne, the station leaders at Wamba. David wrote to Ivor: "Your last letters were nothing short of thrilling: Anne and I would give anything to be able to come to Opienge and witness for ourselves what is going on."

Ivor shared his concern about those who assumed they were filled with the Spirit just because they had been physically shaken. David supported his brother's conclusions and the need for discernment. He said he had learnt to gratefully and joyfully accept all the blessings and movements of the Holy Spirit, but not to put too much trust in experiences themselves, as they would pass. Experiences on their own could not keep a person walking in a way that was pleasing to the Lord.

Not everyone believed the Opienge conference reports carried back to the villages. Non-Christians scoffed at the accounts and derided the Christians who made the claims. As the winds of revival spread not everyone accepted the movement gladly. Some discredited the work of the Lord, saying it was 'Kitawala', a Congolese cult, and the missionaries had given people 'dawa', medicine to make them fall down. Members of another denomination, who looked contemptuously upon HAM's work, were particularly scathing about the reports. Only a personal encounter with the power of the Holy Spirit would convince those opposed to the revival that the reports were true.

21

Revival Spreads to Other Stations

The tornado of blessing blew through other HAM mission stations, including Wamba, Ibambi, Egbita, Nebobongo and Bomili, and later Poko and Malingwia.

In Ibambi revival started gently through the testimony of an evangelist returning from Lubutu, and it brought confession of sin and renewal of relationship to the Lord for some. Other results were practical. For example, progress on the printing shop roof had been slow but once the men renewed their fellowship with the Lord they finished it quickly.

In June Jessie and Jack Scholes visited Opienge where they experienced the revival and saw that God was doing a new thing. On their return they attended the regular Friday evening meeting in the Ibambi Bible School hall along with a hundred believers. After a time of testimony, praise and prayer, Jack shared a little of what he had seen and heard to the south.

Suddenly everyone heard a roar like an approaching hurricane.[1] At first people assumed it was the start of a storm and stewards began to take down the wooden shutters to prevent them being blown inside and injuring people. Some peered outside expecting to see dark clouds and wind-blown palms, but the evening sky was clear and still. Yet inside the lanterns suspended from the ceiling beams shook wildly to and fro, the building rocked as if vibrating in a violent earthquake and the hall filled with the deafening noise of a huge wind. It was, in fact, the presence of the Holy Spirit, falling in great power.

A tremendous clamour began as the people poured out their hearts in loud prayer and praise to God – men, women, boys and girls, were drunk with the Spirit. Many were in tears, shaking beyond their control, some kneeling, some standing, others throwing themselves on the floor, though no one was hurt.

Jack and Jessie were not disturbed, for they knew the Holy Spirit was at work and they were experiencing something similar to the day of Pentecost. Jack moved among the people, speaking quietly to the leaders and missionaries, encouraging them to pray that the Lord would be in control and have the freedom to act as he pleased. Together they endeavoured to assist people where they could, for many were gripped by a deep awareness of their sin, confessing their theft, jealousy, anger, coldness of heart or spiritual pretense.

Once they confessed their sin and received forgiveness they were filled with a remarkable joy. Singing broke out in waves, the words original rather than from known songs, inspired by the Holy Spirit, spontaneously giving praise to the Lord. Some continued worshipping till 2.00am, and even all night. More Christians arrived from the surrounding areas until by Sunday a vast crowd gathered to praise the Lord.

A few days later a team visited neighbouring Nebobongo and the same thing happened there. From all areas letters began to stream into Ibambi telling of similar mighty outpourings of the Spirit. Missionaries asked for prayer to deal with those under conviction of sin, for in listening almost constantly to people confessing they wanted to avoid becoming numbed or immune. In addition they needed godly wisdom to deal with those who grew fanatical.

When the fire first fell at Ibambi some of the Bible school students were away visiting villages. After they heard the news some said with confidence that they had no more sins to confess. However when they returned the Lord met them and they found there were indeed sins to confess, mostly heart sins and family difficulties. Some were in tears and others prostrated themselves on the ground. One woman fell down flat as she confessed her hatred, crying out to God for mercy. The next day she said she had no idea that she had fallen. With the assurance of forgiveness came wonderful joy with the air full of praises to God. The Bible school had a different atmosphere, full of joy and a sense of the presence and the power of the Lord.

The revival spread across the region in the coming months. In July 1953, Eric Smith reported from Egbita, where he and his wife Daisy worked, that they were experiencing revival. In the same month David Davies wrote from Wamba of their revival experiences, saying that the change in lives was almost unbelievable. Confessions ranged from trifling sins to those of the worst kind, the accompanying agony and shame enough to break the hardest heart. God did more in one week, he said, than the missionaries could have accomplished in a thousand years. Friends were reunited, husbands and wives reconciled, hypocrisy and deceit brought to light, backsliders restored, non-Christians saved, and preaching, praying and Bible reading revitalised.

One of the most touching instances of conviction in Wamba was the case of Apanakua, wife of Amboko Jean. She had no shakings but her agony was dreadful, so much so that it almost killed her. Everyone had treated her as the innocent party of her husband's sins and she had maintained that role. But it transpired she had known all about them, even partaking in them. Agony and distress typically resulted when people caught a glimpse of their sinfulness in the light of God's holiness.

Ivor travelled around the villages near Opienge, chauffeured by Aubrey, visiting churches, holding meetings and sharing about the revival. At a village north of Opienge they witnessed manifestations of the Spirit similar to those experienced at the conference. Ivor was blessed at the way Aliasi, the evangelist who had confessed to wrong entries in his report book, ministered to those seeking to renew their relationship with the Lord.

Two childless wives received assurance from the Lord that they would have a child each and were also given their names. Many polygamists were convicted about their marriage situations and a number of unbelievers, some obvious enemies of the church, came to faith in the Lord. The European community was also touched by the events. Belgian officials, Greek shop keepers and Cypriot traders were all amazed, especially at the number of locals who came to confess crimes of theft.

At another village along the same road Christians cried and prayed at length for unbelieving relatives, like Lokamba Meza, who groaned in great agony as he prayed for his brother, a backslider. Tunziako, the wife of an elder, and evangelist Alieni Paulo were both similarly burdened. Alieni prayed broken-hearted for nearly two hours for his sister and for the hardened villages between Opienge and Nderekoko. He continued praying while others carried on the meeting, not affected by them, nor they disturbed by his desperate prayers.

Evangelist Febrieni, at Alieni's side, was filled with the Spirit, stretching out and withdrawing his hands, saying they were heavy with the blessing of the Holy Spirit. Eventually he stood up and spoke, calling on some by name from his village to witness his words. He said the Lord had told him that he was going to do wonderful things there and in nearby villages, including those Alieni had prayed for. Then the whole congregation joined him, praying that his prophecy would come to pass.

At the mission station of Bomili, Ivor, Aubrey, and a team of people from Opienge ministered at a weekend conference. Ivor asked Alimoya, the wife of an Opienge pastor, to give her testimony after his introductory message. She walked up to the pulpit, placed her hands on the railing and opened her mouth to speak, but nothing came out. Instead, she burst into tears. Eight hundred pairs of eyes watched her as the tears streamed down her face and on to her clothing. It was not what Ivor had in mind when he had invited her to speak.

Eventually Ivor went to her side, placed his arm around her shoulder, and guided her back to her seat. He had already spoken to the congregation about the Opienge revival without any detectable impression on his listeners. He thought a personal testimony from someone like Alimoya, who had been wonderfully touched by the Holy Spirit, might break through the hardness of the people.

"Well, we tried, Lord, but no success," he said to himself as he and Alimoya sat down.

They had no sooner taken their seats when the faint sound of weeping broke out in the hall and quickly spread. People began to cry out in agony, trembling, shaking and confessing their sins, with manifestations similar to those at Opienge. Revival had come to the Babari tribe at Bomili.

During the team's visit Alieni Paulo had a remarkable vision. One night he could not sleep and fell into a trance. He heard his name called and saw a revolving wheel in the sky. He was told the aimless revolving of the wheel represented formal faithless prayers, which were of little value. The vision then changed and Alieni saw a great column of smoke ascending and forming a vast cloud which appeared to be driven towards the earth. He was told it represented the prayers of the Spirit-filled believers, forming into a mighty weapon in God's hand, to be used for the good of the nations and for revival. The next day Alieni related his experiences, saying he thought he was in a trance all night, from which he received a wonderful insight into the value of prayer.

Revival did not seem to come to areas simply because of the presence or the testimonies of those already touched by the outpouring of God's Spirit. In most cases the groundwork for revival was laid beforehand through prayer and preparation of the heart. In Bomili's case, weeks prior to the arrival of Ivor's team, God prepared a Congolese evangelist who was convicted about his sin. As he prayed and made confession, the Holy Spirit shook him and anointed him. He experienced a deep burden for the lost, spending entire nights in prayer and praise, but attending to his brick-making work the following day as if he had enjoyed a full night's sleep.

One of the missionaries on the station had laid further groundwork for the revival. She felt that she should pray for the schoolgirls under her charge. One night, while in prayer, she experienced a strange trembling and a pounding heart before a torrent of prayer poured from her, an experience repeated several times before the team arrived. When the Spirit fell at the weekend conference the schoolgirls were among many who were greatly blessed.

The lessons learned initially at Opienge in dealing with unusual manifestations of the Holy Spirit proved invaluable, and enabled Ivor's team to help people come to terms with the events. They encouraged those suffering deep conviction to seek release by confessing their sins, and then to glorify God and ask for the infilling of the Holy Spirit. Any signs of fanaticism were dealt with and the people were encouraged to seek to know God better by reading the scriptures.

In October Ivor attended a meeting of HAM leaders at Malingwia. He found it most interesting to pass through Wamba, Ibambi, Egbita and Poko and to see and hear of the effects of the Lord's working in each place. The church had been revived, backsliders had been brought back to the Lord, and sinners had been converted.

Although it was the work of the same Spirit there seemed to be an individuality in each place. In some places it was the clapping of hands, at another the repeat singing of certain choruses, at another dancing before the Lord, and at another an abundance of hallelujahs. Yet common to all was great joy at the mention of the Lord, and deep concern in prayer over the state of the lost, often accompanied by weeping and crying for their salvation.

There was a common pattern,[2] even in places hundreds of kilometres apart. Firstly, there came a deep conviction of sin and a desperate need to confess everything and make restitution where possible. Then, to those who renewed their relationship with God, and to those who had been praying and believing for revival, there came great joy, such that they were unable to contain it. There followed a burden of prayer for the unsaved and an urgent need to go out and witness to them, teams assertively taking the gospel to surrounding villages in a way not before seen.

However, in spite of the great blessing, there was a constant need for vigilance. On October 1953, Ivor returned to Opienge and discovered all was not well. There had been a disturbing change of mood that had occurred in his absence.

[1] Details of the revival in Ibambi are taken from *This is That: The Spirit of Revival – A first-hand account of the Congo Revival of the 1950s*, edited by Norman Grubb, 2000. Introduction by Helen Roseveare, pages 7-10.

[2] Helen Roseveare, *Living Stones*, page 62

22

Stumbling Blocks to Revival

On his arrival back at the station Ivor sensed a distinct difference in the atmosphere, a cooling off of the passion that marked the early days of revival. The fervour and joy had disappeared and in their place was the return of apathy.

Pastors and evangelists were there to receive their pay and Ivor spoke to a gathering about the difference he noticed, challenging them about hidden sin. The next day he felt the same, so he announced to the leaders that they would meet together in prayer and study of the Bible until the Lord released them. He had no idea what they would experience in the next few days.

Ivor consulted some and found them loathe to talk about the prevailing lethargic atmosphere. After he persisted one spoke up, telling him there was an accusation of adultery against a young pastor. But the individual had denied it. Ivor pressed ahead with his series of prayer and teaching meetings, based on the book of Joshua, beginning with the victory at Jericho.[1] In spite of the theme there was no atmosphere of triumph, and prayer was heavy and laborious. The next day they proceeded to the failure at Ai as a consequence of the sin of Achan.

That evening Elder Matalembo approached Ivor saying that one of the evangelists had come to him greatly troubled, but he did not declare any sin in his life. The next day the study reached the judgment on Achan. During the interval Matalembo brought the young man to Ivor, saying the evangelist had confessed to flagrant sin. At the next session Ivor pleaded with the people to repent of their sin and it was then that the guilty man stood in front of the gathering and confessed his immorality.

There was an immediate and overwhelming reaction.

"What an awful thing, sin, sin, sin. Oh God, forgive us," elder Abele repeated loudly, breaking into uncontrollable crying. The congregation responded with loud sobbing and pleading for forgiveness, such as Ivor had not seen before. Then the Holy Spirit came down on the whole meeting.

In the middle of it all one of the workmen, Alili, arose with one arm upraised and the other fixed straight down to his body.

"My arm is fixed. Look friends, my arm is fixed," he cried out. "Oh, Lord, don't break my arm. Look, friends, my right arm is free and I have joy in my right arm, but oh my left arm, oh, oh, it is breaking. Friends, the Lord tells me my left arm is fixed, for it represents the women's side of the meeting and there is sin among them. Oh, friends, repent, repent!" It was the practice for the women to sit on one side of the church and the men on the other.

Then almost immediately evangelist Febriene fell to the ground with his hand covering his eyes, saying that he had received a vision from the Lord whose eyes were on some in the meeting in anger. He, Febriene, could not look up, he said, for the eyes of the Lord were still there. The fingers of his hand were fixed, similar to Alili's arm. He and Alili were like that for at least an hour and everyone lost sense of the time. But then one after the other came forward or stood up and acknowledged their sin before the congregation.

Alili seemed to have real intuition as to who was concealing sin and what type of sin it was. He kept saying there were two with bitter feelings towards their wives. Sure enough, two men, one of whom was regarded as a model Christian, stood to confess what they had been planning. They wanted their wives to leave them so that each would be free to marry another and then proceed to enter Bible school. Their wives could not achieve the standard set for the school, yet somehow the men were deceived into believing they would be accepted if they acquired new wives.

The confessions continued, with numerous hidden sins exposed. But still Alili and Febriene were not free. Then Elizabeta, wife of evangelist Samueli, crossed over to her husband, spoke to him and left the room.

Alili and Febriene, the two men with fixed limbs, were in terrible pain, at times reduced to screaming. Both Ivor and Aubrey were at a loss as what to do. When Ivor saw Elizabeta leave the room he assumed she went to attend to her children in their accommodation. He turned and pleaded with the pastors' wives to confess if they had done anything wrong.

Elizabeta returned and sat in the front row. After a while Ivor repeated his appeal to the women. Elizabeta stood up.

"It's me," she said. "When the call came for the pastors and wives to collect their salaries at Opienge I was in my village. As I was packing up to come here with my husband, another woman gave me some eggs and told me they were a gift for Mrs Davies. I brought them with us and gave them to Mrs Davies, but she gave me some money for them which I handed to my husband. When I saw the evangelist in pain I realised it was because of the eggs, which were a gift for the Davies, and not to be exchanged for money. I got up, took the money from my husband and returned it to Mrs Davies. I've confessed it to her and we've prayed about it."

After she related her story one man was released but the other was still bound. He said she was not finished and must say how many eggs there were. When she said there were six he immediately came free. It was another case which clearly indicated God's impartiality in dealing with sin. Regardless of whether the people believed the sin was great, as some was, or small, like the eggs, to a Holy God, any sin was untenable.

Many things that Ivor and Rose and their fellow missionaries experienced in the revival were new to them. Some even frightened them, such as the reality of God's view of sin. Ivor searched the scriptures to discover similar events in the Word. He studied the story of Miriam and her leprosy when she criticised her brother Moses, and the story of Ananias and Sapphira and their deceit with money in the early church. Thus he received a new understanding of God's holiness and the need for the fear of the Lord, enabling him to preach about the danger of the anger of God if they ignored sin. Ivor felt a genuine sense of pleasure when he saw people respond with a sensitive humble spirit.

Another lesson Ivor discovered was that when revival fire fell the devil was quick to introduce his counterfeit to frustrate the work of the Holy Spirit. Nowhere was that more evident than at Lubutu, where the revival began. Ivor had been to Lubutu in the early days of the HAM work, and he had heard of the endemic immorality and witnessed the large numbers of men and women regularly drunk throughout the day.

The Lubutu mission station was established in 1937 and over the years many were won to the Lord, brought out of their former lifestyle, and established into a number of village churches. Yet the evil spiritual influences of the past culture were still prevalent. In November 1953 Ivor received a letter from Cyril Taylor, a New Zealander working at Lubutu, expressing concerns about events following the initial revival. Many clung on to the revival, he wrote, as God's special blessing and yet there was no real change in their lives. He discovered some elders to be deceitful, as well as an unpleasant case of immorality which took place while the revival shakes were going on.

One elder in error said he thought it would be good if Cyril returned to his home country because he had hindered the blessing when he asked a young girl to go outside the church while he was preaching. She was experiencing a series of shaking and screaming fits and could not control herself, hindering others from hearing the message. That was the only time he had done that, for he was aware of obstructing the moving of the Holy Spirit, which both Jack Scholes and Norman Grubb warned about. Cyril was concerned his people needed to move from faith in the physical externals of revival to seek the true blessing deep down in their hearts.

Ivor was already aware of similar instances in the Opienge region where he saw the Enemy trying to get people to do things contrary to God's ways. When he pointed out such instances some told him he was thwarting the Spirit of God and they should obey God and not himself as a man. Ivor was initially shocked when he received the accusations but the Lord gave him discernment, and setting aside his fear he pointed out their error in the name of Jesus. He was heartened that there were few wild and difficult individuals and there was a real spirit of prayer among the people. Ivor came to understand that if the activities taking place did not measure up to the spirit of what was written in the Bible they were obviously not of God.

In contrast to the difficulties experienced at Lubutu other stations saw a real change in lives. The problem was that the Lubutu Christians focused too much on the physical manifestations of revival which were merely a means of bringing about repentance. What God then desired was to fill people with his Holy Spirit. Because those in Lubutu did not recognise the need for the infilling of the Spirit they continued to be troubled by sin.

On the positive side, important words of prophecy featured in the revival. One Sunday, in the middle of Ivor's sermon, the Davies' gardener stood up in the centre of the seated congregation. Ivor's sermon was flowing well and the last thing he wanted was an interruption. After attempts to ignore the erect figure Ivor gave up, for he could no longer keep his mind on his notes.

"What is the matter?" he enquired. His gardener was usually a reticent man and not given to making a show of himself in public.

"I had to stand," he replied. "My heart is burning with a message."

"Tell us, brother," said Ivor. "What is on your mind?"

"This blessing is for a reason. Friends, we have to be ready," the gardener began. "The Lord has revealed to me that a great trouble is coming to the Belgian Congo. Many of us are going to die and many are going to suffer. It's going to happen over the whole region and this area in particular where we're living is going to receive a lot of trouble and suffering. We have to be ready." And he sat down.

How could Ivor continue to preach after a message like that? The gardener's prophetic word was not an isolated one. The same theme appeared in other prophecies throughout the country. Ten years later the message was fulfilled when the Simba Uprising resulted in many deaths and much suffering throughout the nation, especially in the church. One of the casualties was missionary Winnie Davies,[2] stationed at Opienge, and many Opienge people were among those who died or were cruelly persecuted. Yet the revival of the 1950s prepared the church to survive the onslaught of incredible horror and evil.

The gardener's prophecy was just one example of the miraculous gifts of the Holy Spirit in the Congo in those years. Healings were another. People were healed during the meetings without specific prayer for them. They came to the front and testified when they were healed, everyone acknowledging the reality of their healing because they were familiar with their illness or injury.

One example involved a teenage schoolgirl who experienced a wonderful filling of the Holy Spirit. She said that when she asked the

Lord to heal her back injury the Holy Spirit gave her the faith to believe, and as she believed a hot burning sensation ran through the affected part, and she was healed.

Visions from the Lord were another regular occurrence. For example, one woman was given a vision of her ears becoming larger and larger, being pulled down by her earrings until they were like elephant ears. The Lord then spoke to her, saying that she wore the earrings to church to draw attention to herself.

Years after leaving the Belgian Congo Ivor reflected on the revival and God's dealings with him. Why had it taken 21 years of Christian service before the Holy Spirit fully empowered him for the task? The answer was not easy or straight-forward.

He recalled his Bible college days and a particular prayer he prayed. The Lord told him to lift his hands and call them holy. Ivor obeyed, despite the fact that in those days no one raised their hands to the Lord in public. His hands quickly felt heavy and he became aware that he had used them for sinful things that did not glorify God, even small things, such as the way he worded a letter to a friend. Thus the Lord showed him that his hands must be clean. Later, he realised that one reason the Spirit did not come down on him at the time was because there were petty things in his life that he should have dealt with.

On the other hand there was also the factor of God's timing and sovereign will in revival. In a magazine article years after the Congo revival Ivor wrote: "For a revival to happen is the sole prerogative of the Lord. It is not necessarily true that if we meet the conditions God will send revival. He moves when, where and how He so desires. Of course, it was prayer, intense and prevailing prayer, which has moved the hand of God in many a renewal or revival. The Welsh Revival was an example. Much prayer and intercession was made for Congo itself before the revival, but ultimately it is God Himself who decides where and when to manifest His power."

Many prayed for revival, he said, but wanted it to happen according to their own ideas or plan. Christians needed to be sensitive to the Holy Spirit and be quick to obey His gentle promptings. God usually dealt with the leaders first. Often it was after the leaders were in tune with God that he had the liberty to work as he wished on a wider level.

It was vitally important that everything that accompanied revival be tested by the Word of God. Prophecies, visions, revelations, works of miracles and manifestations needed to be received in the light of the scriptures because the devil tried to distract and confuse the purpose of God, with a counterfeit for almost every divine work.

In spite of every difficulty Ivor and his missionary colleagues were convinced of the overwhelming value of the revival. In the ensuing years, the church doubled in numbers and then trebled, strong enough to endure and survive the horrors of the civil war.

[1] Joshua chapters 6 and 7

[2] Winnie Davies, not a relative of Ivor, died in the Simba Rebellion in 1967. David Davies, Ivor's brother, recorded her story in *The Captivity and Triumph of Winnie Davies*.

23

The Fixings: Stranger than Fiction

During a Thursday prayer meeting a young girl, Elizabetha, unexpectedly found her little finger curled around her lower teeth and her arm fixed at her shoulder and elbow, pressing against her ribs. She cried out in agony. Ivor asked her what the matter was and if she had done something wrong. She replied that she was bound for two reasons – her own wrongdoing and that of others. She confessed to displeasing the Lord by playing around with some of the boys.

Then at least ten others in the meeting, including one of the Europeans, confessed to grumbling and having a critical attitude. Elizabetha's finger came free but her arm remained fixed, and she said she felt that a person present had not yet admitted their sin. She walked up the aisle, crying and pleading with the Lord not to break her arm, and calling on the person to come clean. She sat down for a moment near a young man, Fanuel. Then she stood up and walked down the aisle to the middle of the church, crying and groaning.

Continuing to pray she lay down on the floor and called the young man by name to put his life right. He stood up and made a partial confession but Elizabetha's arm remained fixed. Ivor asked him if he had more to say, and he stood again, completing his confession. Straightaway Elizabetha's arm became free.

The whole episode took over an hour. The fifty or sixty people in the church prayer meeting were amazed and noted to each other the Lord's displeasure with idle words and actions. Although the girl had been in agony the pain immediately disappeared when she was released, and she was soon sitting among the other girls, giggling with them in typical youthful fashion. That was just one example of a strange phenomenon they experienced during the revival. They called it a 'fixing'.

Some aspects of the revival, like the 'fixings' were not easy to understand. Week after week they witnessed what they later referred to as the 'fixing time'. It took time for Ivor and others to accept them as part of God's working. It seemed the Lord bound people in various ways. Ivor wrote to his brother David telling him he did not understand whether things like the 'fixings' were truly a part of the revival. He understood the presence of sin but the 'fixings' were something he could not fathom. Nor could he find any evidence of them in the Bible.

David replied that his first reaction was one of suspicion, because he had never heard of such things. But he was sure Ivor would not be misled by people acting in the flesh. The only scripture he could think of was the case of Jeroboam's paralysed arm[1] which he could not pull back again. In spite of the lack of scriptural guidance Ivor and others came to see the strange manifestations as part of God's work among them.

One unusual event concerned two schoolgirls. In November 1953, the Davies family were eating their evening meal just as the sun went down when a girl ran into the house.

"Bwana! Come quickly to the girls' compound," she shouted. Ivor called Aubrey from his house and they hurried to the girls' compound. Next to a low wall they found Neema standing with one leg in between the legs of Yosafina who was sitting. Neema could not remove her leg and both girls were crying.

Ivor told Neema to move away and take her leg out. When she wailed that she could not Ivor attempted to lift her away, but instead he lifted both girls who bawled in pain even louder. Then he remembered the incident with Elizabetha and he asked the girls what they had been up to. Neema admitted she had stolen some food and immediately Yosafina's legs opened up and Neema removed her leg. But then Yosafina's legs snapped together. The two missionaries heard her knees and ankles click as they hit each other, and she screamed in pain.

It occurred to Ivor they were in the girls' school and should have their wives with them. Aubrey ran and called the women to join them. Rose asked Yosafina to stand up, but she continued to scream. Ivor told Rose what had happened to Neema, so Rose asked Yosafina if she had done anything wrong. She confessed she had been out with one of the boys and as soon as she did so her legs were released. The whole episode took two and a half hours to be resolved. If both girls had been willing to confess quickly it would have come to an end much sooner.

They saw 'fixings' take place numerous times in different locations, and not confined to sinning Christians. There were reports of non-Christian labourers working in the village cotton fields suddenly being paralysed until they confessed their sin. Others would begin to tremble uncontrollably in their beds at night. David reported a man lapsing into a coma, demonstrating to the locals that resisting the conviction of God had drastic consequences.

At Basaula, only a few kilometres from the Opienge station, an unbeliever named Kapalemba was on his way to his wine palm to drink when he was addressed by a voice. Immediately his legs crossed and failed to unfasten and he was forced to sit on a log. His hands also crossed and seemed to be held together by 'a heat', he said. The voice told him to confess all his sins and in a loud voice he did so. Instantly his legs were released. The voice ordered him to go to the centre of the village and repeat his confession for everyone to hear. As his hands were still locked together he decided it was a good idea to do so. As soon as he completed his confession his hands came free.

Because he did not understand God's dealings with him nor his need of salvation he continued to drink heavily. However, an Opienge elder and his wife, Matiasi and Anna, visited the village, and when they heard of the incident they found Kapalemba and led him and his wife to the Lord.

The resemblance between the paralysis brought on by the 'fixings' and the paralysis caused through the Sumba witchcraft practised in the Opienge district many years earlier must have been confusing for those who could remember it. However, there was a distinct difference between the two: the power of the witchcraft paralysis was broken by prayer, whereas it was only the confession of sin that brought about release from the 'fixings'.

Another example of 'fixings' at Opienge involved an ageing man and his wife, Note and Tiba. They had been asked to consider living in the girls' compound as a surrogate father and mother, to look after the girls who were boarding on the station and attending the school. However Note in particular was reluctant to do so.

Back in 1937 Note and Tiba had no interest in Christianity. They were bound in superstition and afraid of even passing the mission station. However, Note was injured while working on the roads and came to the Opienge station for medical help. Rose was more than willing to provide assistance, provided he attended Christian meetings on the station. Note complied and was converted. Later he joined the station's work force and brought his wife with him, taking up residence on the station.

Over the years the missionaries saw a wonderful transformation in both of them and Note became an elder at one of the village churches. When the Holy Spirit came in revival among the Opienge leaders in May 1953 he was drunk in the Spirit, calling out to Tiba to allow the Spirit to come into her life. Both were radiant when they returned to their village. It was some months later, during a special leaders' meeting at Opienge, that Note and Tiba were asked to help in the girls' compound.

One night, soon after, Note awakened from his sleep. He went outside and on returning to his bed he heard a voice saying, "Don't lie down, pray." He sat on the edge of his bed and prayed, then attempted to lie down, but the voice told him to raise his hands. Note began to argue but the voice ordered him to obey and to fully stretch them up. Immediately his arms locked and he could not bring them down.

"Note, your arms are two and in between is a division," the voice told him. "Now there are two schools at the mission station. I am going to show you that you are to look after one of them. Your arms are fixed but I want you to understand that I want you to do the work of housemaster for the girls. So I will bring your left arm down in a manner that you cannot." His arm began to descend, with the elbow still fixed and only the shoulder joint free. It was as if a heavy weight was pulling his arm down very slowly. When it was horizontal, it was wrenched violently, causing him to be thrown bodily on to the bed.

An amazed Tiba observed everything. When she saw her husband thrown onto the bed she slid off and ran crying to her neighbours that something strange was happening to Note. Meanwhile Note found his arm locked to his side. Crying out in pain he pleaded with the Lord not to kill him, agreeing to do his will and work in the girls' compound. His arms came free and he dashed out of the house, intent on telling Ivor his story. As it was 3.00 am, his neighbours persuaded him not to disturb Ivor at that early hour. At a more respectable time Note related the story.

The next day, when someone described the problem of disobedience in the girls' school Note said he felt the responsibility was his to look after the troublesome girls. It was hardly surprising, in light of

Note's peculiar and compelling experience, that he and Tiba soon assumed the role they had been asked to undertake, and they did an excellent job for a number of years.

Other unusual occurrences took place for which there seemed no rational explanation. One of them occurred at Banginda involving an unbelieving chief. He became angry with the Christians witnessing in front of his house and he threatened them. To vent his antagonism he visited evangelist Alieni Paulo, and while he sat on the verandah, abusing and insulting him, a bee started flying around him, and then a second one.

"What's the matter with these bees? I have no honey on me!" he shouted. In no time a swarm of bees surrounded him and he was forced to escape off the veranda. He continued to insult Alieni from the street, but the bees attacked him again and he ran out to the road 50 yards away. Again he raised his voice to abuse the Christians, and once again the bees made for him until he ran for safety to another of his villages. The Christians were not backward in pointing out to him that the Lord opposed his activities.

Another strange manifestation involved 'holy lights', which many of the Africans declared they saw. On one occasion a light appeared three times in one night in the girls' dormitory at Opienge, described as a yellow light, bright, but not enough to read by. The girls woke the evangelist's wife as well as their teacher and all declared they saw the same thing.

Another time, both Christians and unbelievers saw a 'holy light' glowing in the house of elder Etienne. Others also saw a light appearing in the house of elder Efremu, who lived in the village of Bakoi, north of Opienge. The light appeared three nights running and dimmed if people made a noise. Each time the people quietly prayed. In addition, during special meetings at Banguru, many saw a 'holy light', together with showers of falling starlets. One starlet fell into a woman's cup of tea; the teacup in her hands violently trembled, yet no tea spilled as she drank it.

At the same church Alieni Paulo heard the Spirit tell him to lay his hands on someone, but he was afraid to do so. Then his hands began moving forward of their own accord. He resisted but then clearly heard the Spirit tell him not to be afraid. As he loosed his hands they continued stretching forward. When he stood up, his hands were directed to the head of evangelist, Kapalemba, who was immediately filled with the Holy Spirit.

As bizarre as these accounts might seem the people had no reason to lie about them and they knew all too well the consequences of being deceitful.

[1] 1 Kings 13:4-6

24

The World Hears about the Revival

The children could hardly believe their ears nor contain their joy when Ivor and Rose telephoned them from London in August 1954. Ioan, Miriam and Evan had anticipated their parents' arrival in Britain for several months, but when they finally arrived there was no prior notice. The return came as a shock to Ivor and Rose too. One day they were in the heart of the Ituri Forest and two days later in the middle of London.

Ivor and Rose waited months in Opienge for word from Jack Scholes regarding their departure date. The mission's fund covering furlough fares was insufficient to meet the demand, with the number of missionaries due for leave mounting and everyone having to wait their turn.

It was six and a half long years since the children had seen their parents, boarding those years at The Elms in Arbroath, Scotland. They were keen to be reunited with their parents and frequently questioned them about their return to Britain. On Ivor and Rose's part, another compelling reason to return to Britain was Megan's need for further education. As a ten-year-old she had outgrown her parents' ability to home school her in Opienge.

When notification of their departure came in mid-August they were given only a matter of days to prepare to leave. Instead of travelling by boat they were surprised to discover they would fly home to Britain. They later learned that Jack Scholes accelerated their departure because of a misunderstanding regarding the state of Rose's health. He mistakenly believed the hernia which she coped with for a number of months was in need of an immediate operation.

About the time they departed from Africa, the Davies' considerable contributions to the colony of the Belgian Congo were recognised by King Baudouin of Belgium with official awards. In 1954 Ivor was presented with the Chevalier de l'Ordre de Leopold II, the Knight of the Order of Leopold II, while Rose received La Medaille d'Or de l'Ordre Royal du Lion, the Gold Medal of the Royal Order of the Lion.

Hurried farewells were made to the many Congolese the Davies knew and loved so well. Last minute instructions were relayed to Aubrey and Hulda, who were to oversee the station during their absence. There was insufficient time to write to Britain to notify their children and their wider families of their imminent arrival as they would arrive before the mail.

Little did they know, as they boarded the flight at Stanleyville airport, they would never again set eyes on the country which had been their home for 22 years.

Thirty-four hours later, after short stopovers at Leopoldville, Kano in Nigeria, Rome, and Brussels, they arrived, exhausted but exhilarated.

After such a lengthy separation from their three eldest children Ivor and Rose were keen to spend as much time with them as possible. For the first year back in the UK Megan and Ruth attended school at the Bible College of Wales, which at that time included a primary and secondary school, and the family lived nearby with Ivor's mother and sister, Mamgu (Welsh for grandma) and Aunty Olwen. Ivor's other sister, Aunty Hannah and her husband, Herbert Inkin, lived just a few houses away with the children's cousin Mary. It was a wonderful new experience to have close contact with caring extended family.

Ivor discovered others had alternate plans for him. When they arrived in Wales Norman Grubb, still WEC's home secretary, asked him to speak to Bible schools and universities about the Congo revival. Ivor was reluctant, believing the revival was much too sacred to talk about casually. Norman Grubb was most insistent, saying people needed to understand how God had worked in miraculous ways throughout history and right up to the present day. He was confident that when they heard Ivor's testimony they could then pray and believe that God would move again.

Though torn between his family and his commitments to WEC Ivor agreed to the home secretary's demands and addressed about twenty meetings around Wales. Ivor made it a practice, whenever he preached about the revival, to read and speak from Psalm 24 at the beginning, underlining the need for clean hands and heart before approaching the holiness of God. The success of his addresses was immediately evident, with his audiences amazed by his powerful testimony.

No sooner had he completed those meetings than he was asked to address others all over Great Britain. His travels took him twice the length and breadth of the British Isles, allowing him to spend only short periods of time with his family when his itinerary permitted.

In late 1954, as Ivor was addressing audiences throughout the British Isles, he received letters from several of his HAM colleagues who discounted the revival. Others warned him to be guarded in what he said. Ivor saw the letters as the Enemy's attempt to cause him to doubt what he knew to be true. Although he was certain of what he had experienced and witnessed in the revival the letters nevertheless troubled him.

He expressed his feelings to Jack Scholes who encouraged him by assuring him of the significance of the revival. He said he believed some missionaries in 1953 had actively resisted the spread of the revival or had tried to squash it in their unbelief. People could say what they liked, he said, but he was absolutely convinced that God performed a mighty and genuine work, with the proof of it an on-going reality.

They saw few manifestations now, but, Jack said, the revival had not stopped. The Friday night fellowship meetings were continuing, with testimonies and exhortations from the Word evidence that God was still at work. There was no shortage of those ready to speak and not enough time to hear everyone, the atmosphere continuing to be one of joy and praise, so different from pre-revival days. There was a new understanding of the Word, with the Christians readily accepting any necessary correction.

It was particularly so at the Bible school where the students were able to accept a deeper level of teaching. He was thrilled to see their keenness and their desire to pray. They grew in their understanding so they could readily trust the Lord to supply their individual needs.

"Don't give up because some are not with you. Go ahead and tell what God has done and He will do it again," Jack Scholes wrote to Ivor.

Ivor's brother, David, reported early in 1955 that the 'great excitement' had died down, as he thought it should do, but the fruits of revival, the conversions and the renewals, remained real and obvious. The recent conference at Wamba, with its peace, joy and smooth running was different from anything they had seen before the revival, with people saved at nearly every service. He expected to see vast advances in the church work in the next few years, which would not have been possible apart from the revival.

The letters from Jack and David provided the encouragement that Ivor needed, for he was asked to continue speaking. Next Ivor was sent across the Atlantic for seven months. He visited Canada for two and a half months before travelling through 26 states of the United States. Thousands of people listened to his addresses, with varied responses. Most audiences were deeply moved and amazed by Ivor's accounts, with people convicted of sin renewing their relationship with God.

However, sometimes leaders of the institutions where Ivor spoke did not understand God's work in revival or were afraid of it. In California he spoke at a Bible school on the Spirit's work in the Congo and the students were greatly moved. They started to sing, with one girl in particular taking the lead. Ivor sensed she was attracting attention to herself and he should stop the singing and challenge the students to get right with the Lord. There was a hush and one of the first to break into tears was the girl, who confessed her sin of wanting to be the centre of attraction.

Others followed until one student publicly admitted his hatred against a staff member. There was a long silence before the staff member burst out with his own confession of sin. It was a momentous meeting. But then the vice-president closed the meeting, cutting off what Ivor felt was the work of the Holy Spirit. They had another meeting later but the opportunity had passed and what could have been a greater work did not eventuate.

Ivor did not follow a formula in addressing his audiences but rather listened to the promptings of the Holy Spirit to determine what to say and how to lead a meeting. One common theme in his addresses was the necessity for personal holiness in the Christian walk. Time became irrelevant as people confessed, praised, and worshipped God well into the night.

Ivor learnt lessons as he ministered. Years later he admitted to a friend that he felt at times he overstepped the mark of God's anointing. He came to realise that God gave his anointing for a finite message to a particular audience. He sometimes made the mistake, when his listeners were responding well, of continuing his address beyond that which God had anointed, and God's purposes were lost in the additional words.

In March 1956 Ivor arrived back in Britain from North America, physically and mentally exhausted. The meeting schedule could hardly have been more demanding. Most days included travel, with one or more meetings every day for up to fourteen days in a row. In Canada alone he travelled 19,000 kilometres, mostly by car, and addressed 70 meetings.

A month after Ivor's return from North America he heard reports from the Congo that the revival was still burning bright. In April 1956, at Shabunda, several hundred kilometres south of Lubutu, the spirit of conviction fell during a meeting, with people thrown to the floor, unable to stand until they confessed their sin. At a meeting in Kihembwe over 100 people rushed to the altar crying and pleading for the blood of Jesus to cleanse them from their wrongdoing. Some had visions, not only during the meetings but at night in their homes. Others confessed theft of money and material items and made restitution.

Ivor looked forward to a holiday with his wife and family who lived at The Elms while he travelled. However, people were keen for him to speak at the Christian Literature Crusade's week-long annual meeting[1] in London in May 1956. Ivor accepted the invitation and led the conference's devotions each day with remarkable results speaking, among other things, on Ezekiel's valley of dry bones. The conference discussed only four of the twelve business matters on the agenda because most of the week was spent with people renewing their relationship with the Lord. The devotional times continued for four to six hours each day, mealtimes either ignored or postponed.

At the close of Ivor's message on the second day of the conference one of the leaders stood and confessed the sin of jealousy in her life. Everyone was staggered and broken, weeping with her as she humbled herself before the meeting. Her confession led to a real move of God, and the next day the agenda was abandoned.

People were convicted by the Lord, acknowledging their sin. Confession after confession with much weeping resulted and hardly anyone remained dry-eyed. They confessed their envy, resentments and jealousies, and more than one acknowledged bitter hatred of fellow workers. Such confessions came out only through great travail of soul, and only as a product of the inner working of the Holy Spirit. Some, even after they had confessed, were forced by the Spirit to confess again. Hidden sins, deceits, fleshly passions, all the things they never talked about to each other, were brought into the open.

One young man sobbed and sobbed in agony and desperation over the sin that had dominion over him. Others who had been fighting God for months, even years, despite their outward show of holiness, confessed their sin and repented. Strong men cried and stubborn women wept before the Lord, deeply convicted of their sin, followed by a profound sense of cleansing and God's forgiveness. The agenda ceased to matter.

Coupled with confession and forgiveness was a new feature – the laying on of hands for healing. Ivor and others acted as elders, anointing people with olive oil. At first a few responded to the call but by the end of the week there was a continual stream, as God broke down the former attitudes of prejudice against the laying on of hands. It was not merely a question of obedience to the Word but a new pattern which God was establishing for his people to emulate.

During the conference, as people had confessed their sins, Ivor offered counsel and encouragement. He warned people about the difference between conviction of the Spirit and the condemnation of the Enemy. It was the devil who raked up the past, which they must resist. They were to confess only what the Lord was dealing with at that moment.

After the conference ended Rose received letters from several of the 63 who attended. One lady wrote, "Ivor was God's messenger to us . . . It could not have been easy for him to give the messages he did, seeing that we were supposed to be a body of people already well on the march for God. But he was faithful and God used him. While he was speaking there was rapt attention and time stood still . . ."

Ivor's speaking ministry became widely recognised in Britain and came to the attention of one of England's foremost preachers, Dr Martin Lloyd Jones, who asked Ivor to address a ministers' conference in Wales. When Ivor received the request he was enjoying some time with his family in Arbroath and really wanted to remain with them, but he knew he should accept the invitation. It was a daunting task to address the 80 church ministers but Ivor's message struck home to many who attended.

The WEC report of the conference said: "God broke through . . . it was moving to see young ministers weeping as they put their lives right with the Lord, and to see Martin Lloyd Jones as a father weeping with them."

When Ivor arrived back in Scotland he was exhausted. Though virtually penniless he took his family for a well-deserved holiday. Many years later he confided to a friend that one of his few regrets in life was that he did not even have enough money on that holiday to buy his children some sweets. However the children had no memory of being deprived, remembering only the joy of being on holiday in the company of both their parents.

At the end of June 1956 Ivor embarked on another major speaking tour. Norman Grubb asked him to go to Australia and New Zealand, speaking in churches, Bible colleges and at WEC's Australian conferences. At first Ivor shrank from the idea, feeling inadequate for the task, but the Lord assured him he was in control. The journey by ship to Australia via the Suez Canal proved an eventful one. At the time, President Nasser of Egypt nationalised the Suez Canal which led to an international crisis involving the UK. Ivor's ship was buzzed by Egyptian fighter aircraft and for a while it seemed the ship might be detained.

Ivor's Australian itinerary involved thousands of kilometres of travel through Queensland, New South Wales, Victoria, South Australia and Tasmania. He struggled with mental tiredness, finding it a continual strain to speak and minister at meetings, but Rose and others at home prayed regularly for him. Many came into a right relationship with God, with lives revitalised in renewed trust and obedience.

Rose stayed at the London WEC headquarters, enjoying meeting missionaries as they came and went, as well as the new workers. It enabled her to pray intelligently for them and the work in which they were involved. The Davies children were scattered around Britain. Ioan entered national army service undertaking educational work. Miriam completed her first year of nurse training at the Dundee Royal Infirmary and Evan, Megan and Ruth attended high school.

After a two-week Australian holiday in January 1957 Ivor travelled by plane to Auckland, New Zealand, to begin a three-month series of meetings. When he received news that Rose was to be admitted to hospital for an operation he wanted to fly home. But Rose felt he should not abandon his tour, encouraging him to continue it as planned.

Ivor's revival message came as a surprise to the churches he addressed in New Zealand. People found his preaching about the outpouring of Holy Spirit strange, for even the raising of hands was not seen outside of Pentecostal churches at that time. He met with a group of ministers, Salvation Army officers, Brethren leaders and their wives in what he felt was a significant meeting, especially as they asked pertinent questions about the Christian life and victory over sin.

Ivor's largest meeting was at the Auckland Baptist Tabernacle, where he met Blyth Harper, who in later years became a close friend. About 1000 people packed the church to hear him speak about the revival. His report of the conviction of sin, the joy that followed repentance, the visions he experienced, the miracles God performed, and the waves of blessing that swept from station to station, caught the imagination of individuals. His messages awakened a vision of what God could do and planted seeds of expectation for renewal. Ivor also formed important relationships with men like Leonard Ravenhill, Campbell McAlpine, Arthur Wallis, and Muri Thompson, people like-minded to himself.

Ivor learnt that the local WEC council was keen to find a couple to take up the leadership of the work in New Zealand, establishing a headquarters to prepare local candidates for overseas work. A former missionary to Spanish Guinea, Alec Thorne, had administered the New Zealand work for a number of years but was nearing retirement age. Ivor realised it was possible that he and Rose could be considered for the role, given their mission experience. He was therefore not surprised when Norman Grubb suggested the very thing by letter to him while he was still in New Zealand.

What shocked him, however, was an additional suggestion that Norman made in the same letter.

[1] Christian Literature Crusade or CLC is a ministry which distributes Christian literature world-wide. It was established by WEC but is now a separate organisation.

25

Call to New Zealand

By February 1957 Ivor had spent more than two years addressing audiences all over the world, sacrificing time he desired to spend with his family. Having nearly completed his tour of New Zealand all he wanted to do was return to Britain to be with them. So he was flabbergasted when Norman Grubb asked him, in addition to establishing the WEC headquarters in New Zealand, to stay there and not to return to the UK.

When Ivor responded that his family was in Britain, his children in various stages of schooling, Norman replied that WEC would send them out to New Zealand. Ivor did not agree. He had other relatives such as his mother in Britain and he was weary of travelling the world being separated from his wife and children. He emphasised that the children did not like it at all.

Ivor and Rose did not believe it was wise to rush into making such a change-of-direction decision and they wanted confirmation from the Lord that the position in New Zealand was for them, rather than a return to Africa. They decided they wanted three conditions fulfilled to confirm the shift – an invitation from the New Zealand WEC council, sufficient funds for the family's travel there, and a suitable house in New Zealand for both the WEC headquarters and their own home. In the meantime, Ivor would return to Britain as originally planned.

Norman was convinced they were the couple for the job and he continued to pressure them to accept the position. It would be cheaper for Ivor to stay put and the family to travel to New Zealand. Besides, he suggested Rose's health was not up to the rigours of life in Africa.

Rose was staying at the WEC's London headquarters where the Grubbs also resided. When Norman heard that Ivor and Rose were praying for three confirmations he urged Rose to tell him what they were. When she listed them he said it was action that was needed, not prayer. Rose, however, believed the Lord had spoken to her through Isaiah 52:12: "You shall not go out with haste, nor go by flight, for the Lord will go before you and the God of Israel will be your rear guard."

A few days later Ivor received an invitation from the New Zealand WEC Council to take the leadership position. But he realised that it was not a 'sign' from the Lord, but rather a shrewd move instigated from afar by Norman Grubb.

The following fourteen months were challenging. Ivor returned to Britain in May 1957 and spent his time with Rose at the London headquarters undertaking various tasks. Missionaries returned from the Congo on furlough and questioned him as to whether he had lost his guidance, but Ivor was determined not to move until he felt the go-ahead from the Lord. Having to admit, however, that he and Rose were not sure of God's direction was a humbling experience. The Davies were well aware of the shortage of missionaries in the Belgian Congo, particularly ones with the experience they possessed.

Though they also clearly saw the need for a couple to work in New Zealand to prepare missionary candidates, both felt inadequate for the position. Len Moules[1], who had recently taken over Norman Grubb's position as the WEC international secretary, told Ivor that many had felt that he, Ivor, might have been the future leader in London, and therefore definitely had all the necessary qualities for New Zealand.

Rose was unsure of her ability to run a headquarters, with its focus on missionary candidates, and she worried about the children who were at an age when they needed parental guidance. They were scattered around Britain and she and Ivor had no home base to offer them. Through scripture and various speakers Rose was encouraged to commit the family again to the Lord, confident that he could look after them better than she could.

After a year of praying and waiting for their travel money Ivor and Rose felt it was time for them to be more proactive. By May 1958 they had £300, but required a further £500 to cover the family's fares. They decided to pray for the deadline of the end of July for the necessary funds. If the finance did not arrive they would know the Lord was guiding them not to go to New Zealand. They set the deadline because Megan and Ruth were to begin the new school year in August and they needed to know by then where they would go to school. May and June came and went, with no new finance. Soon the end of July drew near.

In the last week of the month Ivor spoke at the annual conference of the Bible College of Wales in Swansea. In the early hours of 30 July, about 3.30 am, Rose woke from sleep at the London headquarters. She was filled with a deep sense of assurance that God wanted them in New Zealand and that he would get them there. The sense of victory, peace and confidence was so strong that later that day she shared her experience with her colleagues.

In the evening, Jurg Heusser, a young Swiss-German who later became a WEC missionary to Turkish people in Germany, approached Rose with a generous offer. He said God had told him to give the Davies what they needed to get to New Zealand. He had money put aside for Bible school but God was leading him to trust him for his future, and if he gave them £500 he would still have enough for one year's training. His father had done a similar thing some time ago and so would not be surprised. Rose told him to sleep on it and pray again but he said he was certain of his leading and it would make no difference.

When he saw Rose next morning Jurg confirmed his decision. He had been reading about C.T. Studd and his reasons for giving his money away. He would be disobedient if he did not give the money to the Davies. Rose and Jurg prayed together and committed each other to the Lord.

The next day, 1 August 1958, Ivor gave the message at the conference, very aware of the Lord's anointing. Then just as he sat down, still on the platform as the hymn was announced, someone handed him Rose's telegram about the gift of money. As he read it he was filled with amazement and gratitude to the Lord. It was in the same conference hall that the Lord had confirmed his call to the Congo 26 years ago.

Then another miracle took place. The same man who gave Ivor the fare to the Congo in 1932 was at the conference in 1958 and gave him £100 towards the house for the New Zealand headquarters. Ivor was thrilled, filled with assurance and confidence that God was in control. It was worth waiting for.

As Ivor looked for a passage for the family on a ship to New Zealand he and Rose weighed up the consequences of moving half a world away. Once again it meant leaving behind part of their immediate family. Evan (18), Megan (15), and Ruth (13) would travel with them, but Ioan (22), in National Service, and Miriam (20), training to be a nurse, would remain in Britain.

Ivor and Rose, with close relationships with so many people in the Belgian Congo, did not lightly make the decision not to return to Africa. They had mixed feelings and their fellow Congo workers, both national and European, were naturally disappointed. The Davies were also aware of the desperate shortage of personnel, but were confident in the Lord's wisdom and guidance.

On a cold foggy day in December 1958 Ivor, Rose and their three youngest children left London's Waterloo station bound for the coast. A number of friends and family members came to see them depart. Everyone was visibly moved as they sang several hymns and prayed together. When they arrived at Southampton they boarded the aging Dutch passenger liner, MS Sibajak, built in 1926/27, for their journey to New Zealand. Rose, Megan and Ruth took a four-berth cabin with an Australian woman and Ivor and Evan travelled in a six-berth cabin with several other men.

In early January 1959 the ship berthed in Wellington, the capital city of New Zealand.

[1] Len Moules was a son of Frank Moules, of the Railway Mission, and brother of Percy, a HAM missionary in the Congo.

26

Headquarters and Home in Auckland

Priscilla Studd visited New Zealand in 1924, beginning WEC's association with the country, speaking in churches and presenting the challenge to evangelise the unreached parts of the world. By 1933 a prayer group and a WEC council were active in Auckland and later the first New Zealand recruits travelled to Colombia.

When the Davies arrived in January 1959 no WEC headquarters awaited them. Although a house for the headquarters had been a condition of their coming they considered the £100 donation for a house as sufficient endorsement that one would be provided in time. After their ship berthed in Wellington the family travelled to Auckland, the home city of the WEC secretary Alec Thorne whom they had come to replace.

Their first home was in Mt Eden with an elderly couple who were members of the New Zealand WEC Council and the Auckland Baptist Tabernacle. Rose enrolled Megan and Ruth at Auckland Girls' Grammar School and Evan found employment. The three months with the elderly couple proved helpful, enabling them to learn about the Kiwi way-of-life, banking systems and shopping, and to come to terms with modern conveniences such as the telephone. Every time it rang they were afraid to pick it up.

Their second home was provided by a lady who had two houses for sale. She felt led to take them off the market and offer one to the Davies family. It was only for four months but was fully furnished and gave them the freedom of inviting people home who were interested in WEC. Despite having no income they entertained frequently, never running short of food. Every time stocks became low someone arrived with a gift of meat or produce.

The year 1959 was an exciting one for New Zealand. Thousands of people flocked to the Billy Graham Crusade and many made decisions for Christ. Ivor was among the counsellors for people who responded to the altar call in Auckland and Megan and Ruth sang in the choir. Ivor addressed churches and Christian organisations around the nation, challenging them about the WEC work in the Belgian Congo. The story of the revival continued to make an impact and raised awareness of WEC's presence in New Zealand.

Ivor continued searching for a property large enough to serve both as the headquarters and as the Davies' home. In June he received a tempting offer of a house in Palmerston North but after prayer, felt not to accept the offer. The following month the council, of which Ivor was now the leader, decided to pray for a large sum of money. If it was forthcoming before their next meeting it would indicate the headquarters was to be in Auckland.

The following day a woman, who had previously pledged £300 once her house sold, telephoned to say it had sold and she would shortly send the money. The next day another person promised a further £500. Then a few hours before the council met, they received further gifts totalling £1050, making it evident that they were to remain in Auckland.

At the end of July the four months of free rental accommodation came to an end and a lady rang to offer them their third home in Auckland. Six ladies shared a house which they had just had extended, providing two more bedrooms and a small lounge. The six women living in the house not only provided accommodation but regularly prayed for the provision of the headquarters.

Several months went by. Ivor viewed suitable houses and placed an offer on one. It was not accepted. Then Ivor received a phone call from a Mrs Pritchard. They were leaving their house, a church manse, sooner than expected and wondered if it would suit the Davies. The Reverend John Pritchard was the minister of the Auckland Baptist Tabernacle and had been offered a position as lecturer at the Bible Training Institue.[1] The large, six-bedroom Mt Eden house would be ideal for the Davies family and prospective missionaries preparing for overseas work. Ivor had the feeling that God was at work, and he and Rose went to see it,

On Mrs Pritchard's advice Ivor telephoned the secretary of the Baptist Tabernacle Board. Ivor had not purchased a house before and was ignorant of the protocols of negotiating house sales. The secretary assured Ivor he would not be able to afford it though Ivor still enquired about the price. When he heard it would cost at least £5000, he was somewhat nonplussed. It was a lot of money and he knew they had only £4100 in the bank.

"Strangely enough we'll be discussing the house tonight at our board meeting," the secretary said. "If you want to put in an offer go ahead."

"What shall I say?" Ivor said to himself. "Well, he said at least £5000 and we've got £4100."

"Okay," he said, "£4600 is our offer." If they accepted it he and Rose would have to ask the Lord for the extra £500.

"Oh, they'll never accept it," the man replied. "They'll probably turn you down right away. But anyway, I'll put it to the board."

The next morning the secretary phoned back.

"They've accepted your offer," he said. How much deposit can you put down?"

"What's the usual amount?" Ivor asked him.

"It's normally ten percent of the full price," he said.

"Well, we've got £4100 in cash," Ivor replied.

"What!" he exclaimed. "Come and get the key. What terms do you want on the other £500? Three months?"

Ivor felt his confidence growing, so he offered one month.

The family moved in. The first and second months went by without £500 coming in and Ivor and Rose began feeling uncomfortable. When Ivor approached the secretary he said he had stipulated three months, so three months it was, even though Ivor had offered a month. At the end of three months they received the money and Ivor made the full payment.

The Henley Road property was dedicated on Saturday 7 November 1959, with 140 people packing the downstairs area – the lounge, the hall, the stairwell, the bedroom opposite the lounge and the verandah.

Ivor and Rose had high hopes for their future ministry now they had their headquarters. They could now hold residential candidate orientation courses to prepare prospective missionaries for overseas service. But as the months passed no New Zealand candidates applied, and in three years they received just one missionary candidate whom they turned down. She wanted to go to Zaire, as it was called then, but she had health issues, with a rash that flared up in the tropics. She kept returning to them and, four years later, went to Colombia.

Ivor and Rose began to wonder why they were there. It was not for want of effort on their part that candidates were not forthcoming. Ivor spoke at meetings up and down the country about the work and the Congo Revival. Rose kept busy hosting people interested in the work. They began to realise that God did have a purpose for the apparent unfruitful period. They travelled and spoke throughout the country, getting to know it well – the people, the ministers and the Bible colleges. In time God would send them candidates.

By the end of 1962 Ivor and Rose had their first intake of prospective missionaries to guide through the candidate course, which not only helped prepare them but also enabled the Davies to assess their suitability for cross-cultural mission work. Candidates lived with them for four months after completing their Bible school training, during which time they grew to know each other, an excellent foundation for future mission relationships.

Ivor and Rose had 22 years of spiritual and practical experience, a superb basis for preparing future missionaries. They personally knew the struggles new missionaries faced in unfamiliar cultures overseas far away from their former homes. Even after candidates departed and began their mission work they wrote to seek the wise counsel of Ivor and Rose.

The Davies enjoyed a sense of fulfilment in their new position. But their joy and satisfaction diminished when they received disturbing news from friends in the Belgian Congo. Though they anticipated political change, no one foresaw the devastating repercussions that change would bring, particularly to the Christian community.

[1] Renamed the Bible College of New Zealand in 1972 and Laidlaw College in 2008.

27

Crisis in the Congo

On Sunday 4 January 1959 riots erupted in Leopoldville, several hundred kilometres from Opienge. It was rumoured that the colonial government refused to permit a political rally in the city. In response unemployed youths went on the rampage, killing people, burning hospitals, schools and churches, and pillaging shops. As they ran through the city streets they yelled 'uhuru' – 'freedom', 'independence', which they sought from the whites.

Official figures recorded 49 Africans died but there may have been as many as 500. Later, January 4 became the Day of the Martyrs, celebrated annually as a national public holiday. In 1959, however, the Belgian Congo was ill prepared for the modern age and its demands of nationalism and independence.

The outburst of vehement nationalism had been building for some years but stemmed directly from political events the previous year. In August 1958 General de Gaulle of France offered independence to any French colony that desired it. The Congolese took up the cry for Belgium to follow suit.

The same year a number of political parties competing for popular support were formed, including the Alliance des Bakongo (ABAKO), led by Joseph Kasa-Vubu, and the Mouvement National Congolais (MNC), led by Patrice Lumumba. With his powerful speeches and his vision for an independent Congo ruled by an indigenous central government, Lumumba won the backing of the majority of the indigenous population.

In October 1959 further riots in Stanleyville sparked an exodus of Europeans, especially women and children. In an attempt to restore order in the colony the Belgian government called a conference in Brussels which Congolese political leaders and provincial chiefs attended. Their delegates rejected outright the Belgian government's ill-considered proposal to offer independence in 35 years' time. Consequently, the Belgians were forced to reduce the proposed preparation period for liberation to six months, with full independence to be granted at the end of June 1960. The Congolese were overjoyed, unaware of the dire consequences of the sudden changes, for which there was a complete lack of essential preparation.

While these political manoeuvres were taking place the work of HAM continued much as it had before. After Ivor and Rose's departure from Opienge in 1954 Aubrey and Hulda Brown assumed responsibility of the mission station. In 1955 they were joined by another colleague, Winnie Davies, who by coincidence shared the same surname and nationality as Ivor. Winnie was a qualified midwife, involved in HAM since 1946. During her years at Opienge she expanded Rose's medical work by establishing a modern ten-bed maternity block and a fourteen-bed hospital, as well as a dispensary which catered for 200 people.

The Browns and their three children departed for furlough in December 1959. Although they were reluctant to leave Winnie on her own, Alieni Paulo, now the pastor of the Opienge church, gave his assurance that he would look after her.

In early 1960 further disturbing indications of things to come occurred. Lumumba had tremendous support in the region, the Orientale Province, and his supporters began visiting factories, shops and mission stations to interview workers, compiling blacklists of employers accused of mistreating their employees. Cars with loudspeakers travelled through towns and villages, declaring the names of those who had been added to the list. Missionaries, including

Winnie, received uninvited calls to their houses from Lumumba's men, behaving in an intimidating and abusive manner.

Rose's sister Daisy, stationed with her husband Eric Smith at Nala, wrote to Rose in April 1960 saying they did not feel that they had much longer there. The situation was changing rapidly, with fresh developments every day. The unrest swelled the flow of Europeans packing up and returning to Europe, with an increase of unemployment and instability. It also left an open door for communists to infiltrate and take charge.

As Independence Day and the elections for the provincial candidates approached feelings ran high between parties. Suspicion and lies were rife and politicians made grandiose promises, stirring up the people. Tribe was divided against tribe, and party against party.

Life became very difficult for the missionaries. Some were accused of mishandling funds, seen also in other emergent African nations. It was not difficult to blacken a character, with many believing the lies and half-truths. Eric Smith wrote to Ivor saying that there was little trust in the missionaries and they felt their work was finished. In the fast changing political environment they needed discernment to know how to handle each new challenge. There was even an expectation of imminent bloodshed.

Some Congolese accused HAM of treating them badly in relation to their schools, for the mission had a policy of not accepting government subsidies. However, missions that received subsidies were not exempt from criticism, or from having difficult demands put on them.

The tensions in the country caused serious problems inside the Congolese church, with increasing mistrust between Africans and missionaries. Disputes led to splinter groups pulling away from churches assoicated with HAM to form their own fellowships. The first problem occurred in the north when one tribe insisted that they should have their own separate mission station at Gamba, rather than share the Nala station with another tribe. The HAM committee turned down the tribe's proposal, with the result that they withdrew from HAM, taking with them twenty churches and their elders and evangelists. Three HAM missionaries went with them, forming a separate mission organisation.

The second major dissension occurred in the south at Lubutu. While the resident missionaries were on furlough a Rwandan so-called pastor, an impostor, came into the area sowing seeds of dissension among the elders. He claimed to be a Christian leader but his assertion was not backed up by letters of recommendation. He alleged the missionaries were holding back funds sent from Europe for the Africans and were using the money for themselves.

Half the church elders believed him and broke away from the Lubutu Church, forming a new group under the leadership of the self-styled pastor. At a special conference twenty elders left the meeting with threats of bringing accusations against the missionaries before the Congolese government. They also refused to hand in their letters of authority given to them by the church.

The picture was not all negative. The returning missionary family received a warm welcome and a number of teachers and elders remained supportive. However, with their area under military control because of the political unrest, rumours circulated as to what would happen when the country attained independence.

The Opienge church also had problems. The HAM committee intended to post a missionary family to Opienge to assist Winnie Davies. However, the Opienge Christians strongly objected, preferring either childless couples or single individuals as missionaries. They reasoned that missionaries with children were preoccupied looking after their offspring rather than the mission work.

Ivor wrote to the Opienge church leaders, recommending the family and encouraging the church to accept them. The Opienge

Christians had always looked upon Ivor as a father, so he expected them to accept his advice. However, their response to his letter was startling and out of character. Marjorie Cheverton, temporarily stationed at Opienge, wrote to Ivor telling him that his letter did nothing but mischief, for the people were affronted at his request. In the atmosphere of approaching independence it was impossible for Europeans to give advice or say anything without being reported or being told that the devil had got into them.

Patrice Lumumba promised that missions would be allowed to continue after independence, but the missionaries wondered for how long, given likely pressure from outside sources. Though it seemed their work in the Congo might be finished they saw it as not necessarily a bad thing, for the church was functioning and running its own affairs. Without the missionaries they would grow stronger and shoulder their responsibilities with more certainty.

Many Congolese had unrealistic expectations of what independence for their country would mean personally. They believed they would have freedom from the tyranny of the white man, their Belgian rulers and, as a result, plenty of money would somehow materialise. However, they failed to realise, as some missionaries feared, that their own masters would be more ruthless than the Belgians had been.

Eric related a small but disturbing incident one night on his Nala station that typified their naive outlook and anticipation of being able to demand what they wanted. A school boy was dismissed from the school after he was caught in the girls' dormitory and he responded by telling the other boys they had all been dismissed. The result was a riot on the station. The boys threatened to kill the Congolese school teacher and to put an arrow through Eric. When things quietened down Eric wrote that the boys expected independence would enable them to visit and cavort with the girls whenever they chose.

Everyone, missionaries and the general population, braced themselves for the worst, as Independence Day dawned on 30 June in the newly-formed country of the Democratic Republic of Congo. Patrice Lumumba was elected prime minister and Joseph Kasa-vubu president. Initially there was peace, but it was short lived, and tribalism and quests for power quickly erupted. Within a month the Congolese army, the Force Publique, after being denied the promise of better conditions given to other public servants, revolted in six provinces and went on a rampage of rape and pillage.

The country was thrown into chaos and within a week more than 40,000 Europeans fled. Because of their isolation many HAM missionaries were initially oblivious of the events taking place around them. Winnie Davies was the first to be alerted at Opienge by Greek traders who lived down the road. They convinced her to join them in a convoy of cars headed for the airport at Paulis. Hours later she pulled her car out of the convoy as it passed the Wamba station and was surprised to discover the station functioning as normal. After she alerted the station's leader, Ivor's brother David, they consulted the local government administrator who advised the evacuation of all women and children. He understood troops at the nearby Watsa Camp had revolted and were moving in their direction.

Missionaries from other northern HAM stations were called together and informed of the situation. Field leader Jack Scholes reaffirmed that all women and children should leave the country but individual adults were free to choose, as they felt led by God. A party of missionaries and children headed in a convoy of vehicles for the Paulis airport. When they found their escape cut off they made a dash for the border and, after a twenty-hour journey, reached safety in Uganda. Huge camps had been established by the Red Cross to feed and shelter the thousands of refugees who poured daily into Uganda from its troubled neighbour.

Not all Europeans evacuated from the country, some electing to stay during the army revolt to continue their work. In fact, some even entered the Congo. Dr. Helen Roseveare had arrived in the Congo in 1953, working first in Ibambi and then in the maternity and leprosy centre of Nebobongo. The Africans called her Mama Luka – they entitled every older woman Mama and Luka was named after Luke, the doctor and writer in the New Testament. Dr Roseveare arrived back in the country from furlough just as the trouble began. Border guards were amazed that while thousands were fleeing to Uganda she was entering the country.

By August the HAM missionaries sheltering in Uganda believed it was safe to return but, once back, found there was less confidence in them because they had left.

Whites now had to carry travel passes. One missionary, Frank Bates, a young Australian, was temporarily held as a prisoner. When he met a road block his captors accused him of carrying a forged pass and confiscated his shoes, shirt, and hat. They forced him to cut grass on the road side and to carry rubbish. Later his abductors decided to take him to Paulis in their car, stopping on the way at every village to parade their catch and tell the people what a corrupt man he was.

Fortunately the driver, who was also the interpreter, told the people that he was a missionary and a decent man, which limited the harassment they had planned for him. The driver also found some sandwiches for Frank to eat during the nine-hour journey of 80 kilometres. When they arrived at the administration office the official, to Frank's great relief, released him, for he was the one who had originally issued his pass, and he had Frank's captors put in prison and whipped.

Several other missionaries were also hassled. Mary Harrison and Muriel Harman, both older women, were imprisoned for thirty two hours and forced to undertake hard labour with the ordinary prisoners, but were then released. Such incidents led to the decision to evacuate Opienge and move to Ibambi or Nebobongo.

The political scene continued to change rapidly. President Kasa-vubu attempted to dismiss his rival Lumumba from office, less than three months after he became prime minister. Lumumba resisted but was forcibly removed in September 1960 in an army coup led by Colonel Joseph-Desire Mobutu,[1] thus beginning his 36-year dicta-torial reign. Meanwhile, Lumumba, who had fled after his dismissal from office, was captured and executed in early 1961.

The number of HAM missionaries remaining in the Congo contin-ued to decline. Despite the crisis, Jack Scholes saw the situation as an advance for the African church rather than a retrenchment. The stations with no resident missionaries continued faithfully, apart from the maternity work. Near Opienge the Angumu mines closed down after Independence Day and the Angumu Road which served both the mission station and the mines fell into disrepair, but the station itself was in excellent condition. The local evangelists gener-ously forfeited their wages in order to pay the teachers to keep the schools going.

Jack reasoned in a letter to Ivor, "Sometimes the local leaders don't ask for counsel, and we must not be hurt by that, for they are grow-ing up and want to make their own decisions. Maybe they do things in a way we would not approve of. We have probably done things in our Western way that they haven't approved either, but they have had the grace to keep quiet. More and more we must trust them to the Holy Spirit to lead, teach, train and guide. They will make mis-takes as we all have done, but will learn by them."

Ivor heard there was a marked improvement in the attitude of the pastors and teachers. Before independence they had grown some-what arrogant. But like so many they modified their attitudes when their visions of utopia did not materialise. The opportunities to preach the gospel remained wide open, but things changed, with the missionaries evangelising the villages and the Congolese in charge of the stations and schools.

Winnie Davies returned from furlough in October 1961. Because of the unrest mission leaders were reluctant to allow her to return to Opienge by herself as she wished, but in the end relented.

The political scene continued in a volatile state, with much uncertainty as to the country's future. The departure of the Belgians left the country with no experienced or educated administrators and many thriving industries ground to a halt for want of trained management staff. Struggles for political ascendancy continued among the tribal factions after the murder of Patrice Lumumba and the removal of his political party from power.

For many Congolese independence meant the removal of all restraints, throwing over all discipline and living as they pleased.[2] One faction in particular, the Simba rebels, a pro-Lumumba group, expanded in the southern regions of the country, motivated by an intense hatred of both whites and national Christians. Through violent action they signalled their intention to stop at nothing in their bid to topple the new government.

[1] Mobutu Sese Seko embarked on a campaign of Africanisation, initially bringing stability but ruling with an iron fist. He turned corruption and the squandering of state resources into an art form, named Kleptocracy and, by the early 1990s, brought economic collapse to Zaire, as he named his country. He remained in power till 1997.

[2] Helen Roseveare, *Give Me This Mountain*, page 138.

28

The Simba Uprising

Ivor and Rose heard the news from Africa in late 1964 with shock and horror. Four HAM missionaries had been murdered. It was revealed later that a fifth member of their team also died violently. The devastating news rocked the whole western world. The whereabouts of others was unknown and casualties among the Congolese, Christians and non-Christians, impossible to calculate.

All the reports from the civil war continued to be deeply disturbing. As news filtered through it became apparent that rebel insurgents in the former Belgian Congo had murdered a number of missionaries, other Europeans and thousands of nationals. In total, between 1960 and 1965, over 30 foreign protestant missionaries died in violent circumstances,[1] as well as a number of priests and nuns. It was estimated that at least 20,000 Africans were executed by rebels, with tens of thousands also killed during the suppression of the rebellion.[2]

The rebels, many of them followers of the assassinated Patrice Lumumba, named themselves Simbas, meaning 'lions' in Swahili. Under a few well-trained and indoctrinated leaders the youthful rebels, known as the Jeunesse, some as young as nine years old, were trained in secret camps to the south of the HAM area. In the breakup of law and order and effective security they reverted to age-old customs of witchcraft and cannibalism, regarding their revived practices as the 'sacraments' of a new 'fellowship'.[3]

Though they lacked organisation and coherence they took over the township of Kindu in August 1964 and moved quickly north, leaving a trail of dead bodies and terrorised people, rioting, looting and burning villages as they went. Besides guns, spears and bows and arrows they were armed with their beliefs in witchcraft, which their leader, Christophe Gbenye, promised would turn their opponents' bullets into water.

Before rebels arrived in a region they would terrify government troops with telegrams, warning what would happen to them and forcing them to flee. People in government employment were murdered without question, as were the educated and the well-off. Unwelcome attention also fell on the churches and foreign missionaries, rebels promising that 'God's people' would suffer after they had dealt with government soldiers. The results were inhumane treatment and massacres of local Christians and foreigners, missionaries and business people alike. Yet through the whole eighteen months of chaos and terror the church grew, many congregations more than doubling.[4]

The young rebels earnestly believed their cause would usher in a new grand era for the Congo. At times they showed kindness and consideration to the missionaries, yet so feared their leaders they would do anything to please them. As an occupying force they were usually brutal and coarse, rough and domineering, their language threatening and obscene. Often drunk, they were liberal with the butt-end of rifles and rubber truncheons. Destruction became a way of life. When missionaries returned after the uprising was quelled in 1966 they found rebels had destroyed up to 90 percent of mission infrastructure in rebel-held areas.

Ivor heard nothing of missionary activity for weeks. Then he received news that Jim and Ida Grainger, working at Lubutu, had been rescued by Congolese troops just as they were being led out to be shot. Others seemed to be safe and well. But soon afterwards they heard of the reign of terror of the insurgent forces. The rebels took over much of the area where WEC had been working for over 40 years – Wamba, Ibambi, Opienge, Lubutu, Lowa and other stations.

A number of missionaries experienced vicious mistreatment while others forfeited their lives.

The personal stories of just a few of the missionaries illustrate the trauma of their ordeal. On 15 August 1964 the rebels took control of Nebobongo, and Helen Roseveare and nine other Protestant missionaries were put under house arrest, suffering in captivity for the next five months.

On the night of 29 October, there was hammering on Helen's door and seven or eight men rushed in, their eyes full of hate, searching for radios and cassette players. Not believing her denial that she had any they ransacked the house before leaving, all except for one. Aware of his evil intentions Helen rushed out of the house and hid in the bushes.

He found her, kicked and hit her, holding a pistol to her head, demanding she declare Patrice Lumumba to be the saviour of the world. She refused and her ordeal culminated in a brutal rape. In the middle of her overwhelming fear and numb horror – where she was yelled at, insulted and cursed – somehow there was the knowledge that God was in control. Later she came to the realisation that it was a privilege to suffer for the Lord.[5]

Over the next few months she and her fellow prisoners were taken to different places in the forest away from advancing government troops. Again and again they thought they would die. At Ibambi Helen was given a mock trial and asked who had beaten her up – so badly in fact, that she could hardly see. The soldiers gathered around her about 800 men who at a certain point were to call out that she was a liar and demand her death. To her amazement she heard 800 men break down and cry, sweeping forward and declaring she was theirs, their doctor.

The struggle with fear was very real for all the prisoners. During the months of capture David and Anne Davies expected to be killed any moment, day or night. On one occasion David was paraded in front of a group of drugged and drunk rebels, each clasping their guns and machetes.

"White man, you're going to die today," they said,

David did not fear death itself, for he knew he belonged to the Lord. It was the process of death, how he died and what they might do to his wife. The tight tension of paralyzing fear built up within him, for he knew how others had died. Gradually he came to the point of release. If suffering was the will of God for him, then it was good.

He told the Lord, "With all my heart I embrace your will; your will be done." The fear snapped and lifted, and a cloud of peace enveloped him.

One particular journey proved to be a dreadful experience for the group and again they all expected to die, especially Jack Scholes, in his mid-60s, who had a spear prodded into his neck. The driver repeatedly delayed his travels. Later, they realised why. He wanted to arrive after dark when there would be no one around to watch the intended killings.

The men were sent to the monastery and the women to the convent, with the threat that they would be killed at dawn. But next morning, for some reason, the commander's orders were not carried out. In late December 1964 white mercenaries rescued Helen and her colleagues in the jungle. They were hardly able to comprehend they were alive and safe after their harrowing ordeal.

Mary Harrison and Muriel Harman were among the missionaries living at the HAM station of Lowa on the Lowalaba River on the upper reaches of the Congo River. Some months before the Simbas arrived in the area, the Lord spoke to Mary from Job 2. 4: all that a man has will he give for his life. Little did they realise that soon they would be forced to hand over food, money and clothes, all that the Simbas demanded in order to preserve their earthly lives. The daily routine of station life was constantly interrupted as the Simbas paid them visits, claiming whatever took their eyes.

On 9 November they were arrested, taken by canoe across the river and interned, suffering mistreatment and beatings with rubber truncheons. Later, two Government helicopters arrived at the mission station to evacuate them, but they were too late.

The rebels took their captives by motor boat to Ponthierville where the mistreatment continued, the prisoners stripped to their pants and beaten. From there they continued by train to Stanleyville, stopping on the way at each station to be met by terrifying mobs carrying weapons and flaming torches. They were imprisoned on the east side of the Congo River, together with some Roman Catholic sisters and priests and three white civilians. They were surrounded by heavy fighting, with the national army shooting across the river at the rebels. Several days later the army gained control of the western side of Stanleyville.

Most of the prisoners were forced into a dungeon-like basement. Seventy one-year-old Mary Harrison suffered several falls, firstly injuring her wrist, then falling three feet down a manhole on to a cement floor, breaking her right leg. The rebels then kicked her in the face and chest, breaking her jaw and ribs. All night she and Muriel and the other prisoners crouched in fear in their underground shelter, without water or sanitary arrangements.

The next day, 25 November 1964, the rebels returned and with menacing orders, manhandled the prisoners up to the top floor of the building, leaving behind Mary with her broken leg, and other injured hostages. They hustled the prisoners into a long room and shot them. Muriel Harman,[6] in her early 60s, was among the dead.

That night and all the following day the few survivors, including Mary Harrison, in constant pain, were alone on the bare basement floor. The next morning white mercenaries mounted a mercy raid across the river, rescuing them and flying them to Elisabethville's Reine Elisabeth Hospital in the south[7] and from there to the United Kingdom.

In time, news filtered through concerning Bill McChesney and Jim Rodgers who also both died on 25 November. Bill, from Arizona, was only 28 years old, having arrived in the Congo in 1960, just prior to Independence. As an American citizen he was the recipient of particularly antagonistic mistreatment, for American soldiers were involved in fighting the rebels and in rescue attempts. He was arrested at Ibambi where he was working and was severely beaten. From there he was taken to Wamba, interrogated and placed under house arrest. Forty-five-year-old Scotsman, Jim Rodgers, teaching in Wamba, took care of Bill, who was suffering the effects of his brutal treatment, as well as malaria.

In spite of his house arrest Bill was allowed to join the mission station evening prayers. One night he said, "Listen brothers and sisters, if you want to live in peace, take your minds off the things of the world. This is a time of death. Do not hold on to your possessions." Later, the truth of those words became very important to the Christian nationals as they hid from the rebels in the forest, with virtually no clothing or food or shelter.[8]

Shortly after, all the white males were herded together and their nationalities demanded of them, with all Americans and Belgians condemned to die. Jim made the decision to stick with Bill, and both were murdered together by the rebels, likely trampled to death and their bodies thrown in the Wamba River. Jim could have saved himself by admitting that he was a British citizen and not an American like Bill, but he chose to stay and die with his wounded colleague.

The next news that reached Ivor was of the possible death of New Zealander Pat Holdaway at Wamba where other HAM missionaries had died. There were only slender hopes of some of them being alive as others saw Pat there before the killing and believed that no white person had escaped. Pat had been working in the Congo for many years, engaged in maternity and general nursing at Bomili. It was a harrowing time, both for those in the rebel-held areas and for those waiting for news, for they heard continual reports of the wholesale slaughter of church leaders and other Christians and knew a number of missionary families were unaccounted for.

Later in November, the New Zealand External Affairs Department telephoned Ivor with the news of those who had died and the rescue of others. As he absorbed the dreadful news he recalled the amazing prophetic message given by his African gardener during revival stating that the blessing was God's preparation for serious trouble in days ahead.

Meanwhile, Ivor and Rose had not heard from Winnie Davies[9] for some months, her last letter indicating no sign of trouble in her area. Rather she wrote that all Opienge sent their love to Bwana Kumi as their Baba in the faith. However, only days after she wrote four local Greek traders and a Catholic priest arrived to warn Winnie that the Simbas were on their way to Opienge and they advised her to accompany them to the safety of Stanleyville.

But she refused. Four years' earlier, during the troubles after Independence Day, she had fled from Opienge. When she returned a year later the Christians had gently rebuked her.

"Why did you leave us when we most needed you? Couldn't the Lord have cared for you as well as us?" they said. She vowed to them that if trouble came again she would not leave them. And although they agreed that she should now escape Winnie was determined to remain with them, whatever the outcome.

On 14 August 1964, the Simbas arrived at Opienge and threatened to shoot Winnie with an arrow. Pastor Alieni Paulo with great bravery thrust himself in front of her and prevented them from harming her. Over the ensuing months the Opienge Church suffered much distress and pain, just as the prophecy ten years earlier stated. Many were terrorised by the Simbas and some were killed but the Christians faithfully protected Winnie, often putting their own lives at risk. Winnie continued her medical work as best she could in the difficult circumstances.

Sometime later rebels compelled her to accompany them as a hostage, and for 33 months they demanded she use her medical skills as they played a deadly cat-and-mouse game with government soldiers in the jungle. Throughout her captivity Winnie continued to serve all who needed her skill as a nurse or a midwife, irrespective of their creed or politics.

Finally a government patrol caught up with the rebels holding both Winnie and Reverend Father Alphonse Strijbosch, a Dutch Roman Catholic missionary, as they were being force-marched in a column in a vain attempt to escape capture. The patrol attacked the rebels, attempting to liberate the missionaries, rescuing the priest, but failing to save Winnie. Though rebel General Ngalo had given her some protection from his soldiers it seems he shot her in the end because of her inability, in her exhaustion, to keep up with the escaping guerillas.[10] Aged 51, she died on Sunday 28 May 1967 at the hands of the Simbas, only minutes before she could have been released.[11]

Ivor and Rose ensured that the New Zealand HAM missionaries were well cared for, as one by one they were evacuated and brought back home. The New Zealand public and the government showed great generosity to the returning missionaries who left Africa with only the clothes they wore. Donations, telephone calls and letters poured in for them.

Ivor received a lengthy telegram from the Prime Minister, Keith Holyoake, expressing the government's sincere condolences for the HAM missionaries who had died. They also pledged to pay the airfares for the returning New Zealanders, cut through the red tape and immediately provide them with pensions.

Christmas 1964 for the Davies was a worrying time as they and many others around the world awaited news of those still unaccounted for. Ivor collapsed during a church service one morning, which his doctor said was probably caused by the stress of overwork and concern for friends in the Democratic Republic of the Congo.

They were most relieved to finally learn of the rescue of Pat Holdaway who was repatriated to New Zealand. Other WEC missionaries whose whereabouts were previously unknown were found to be alive and safe. Many of them, along with hundreds of whites, were rescued by Belgians flying American planes, flown in specifically to evacuate foreigners under threat.

Some years later, when Pastor Idoti[12] from the church in Wamba visited the UK, Ivor and his brother David learnt details of what happened to many of the national Christians after the Europeans were evacuated.

The Simba commander in Wamba called the Christians together, telling them that the whites had brought God to the country, but now they had gone they had taken God with them. Christianity was finished and anyone with a Bible would be shot. The Christians returned to their villages, refusing to deny what God had done for them, deciding to die rather than turn their backs on him.

When the commander heard they were continuing to hold their church meetings he was furious. He had his soldiers surround the Christian homes at dawn and force them to either join the rebels or escape into the forest, taking nothing with them – no clothes, food or bedding. For Idoti it was a terrible moment. He gathered his wife and children, grabbed his Bible, pushing it under his shirt so it could not be seen, and they ran for their lives. Some Christians reluctantly joined the rebel cause but many others refused and, like Idoti, paid the price.

The Bible became their only comfort, speaking faith, hope and courage. Weeks later he was encouraged to find other Christians had also taken their Bibles with them. They hid them, wrapped in cloths, in earthen pots, which they buried in the ground. In the evenings when the Simbas were in their huts they took them out and shared the Word, which seemed to be written just for them, about God who was their refuge and strength, their present help in times of trouble.

The nights in the vast thick forests were very cold. They huddled together, remembering the words of Bill McChesney. Their possessions were gone and they had nothing but the value of their lives in God. Hunger, exposure and illness took their toll and many died, especially among the children and the elderly. Food was a huge problem but friendly pygmies introduced them to edible fruits, roots and leaves, and they caught fish and trapped animals.

Some experienced miraculous deliverance. At a tribunal one elderly pastor offered his life in place of an arrested and condemned young pastor. The commandant was so moved that he ordered a re-examination of the evidence. When the accusations proved false both men were allowed to go free. But God did not reward every case of courage and faith with rescue, and many others lost their lives.

Idoti and his family survived nineteen months in the forest. It was wonderful when they heard the heavy lorries of the national army on the road and realised that the days of the Simba rebellion were at an end. They were given a ride into Wamba, meeting up with other Christians who had made their way out of the forest. But they all returned weak, exhausted, and ill, to find the mission station and their villages in a state of complete devastation. It was only as they gathered together to pray and sing that God lifted their spirits to begin the rebuilding process.

Nationwide, the Simba Uprising was eventually crushed, but not before a terrible death toll, with many Christians among the dead. There is no doubt, however, that the revival of 1953-54 enabled Christians like Idoti and the church to stand firm and to survive during the very difficult times of civil unrest. In the following years many of those blessed during the revival became dedicated and effective leaders of the church.

[1] Colin Whittaker, *Great Revivals*, page 115

[2] 392 Europeans were recorded as losing their lives. Simba Rebellion, Wikipedia.

[3] Len Moules, *This is No Accident: Testimonies of a Trial of Faith in Congo*, page 3

[4] Helen Roseveare, *Digging Dtiches*, page 14

[5] See the film: *Mama Luka Comes Home* – Cross TV – www.cross.tv/78482

In 1989 Helen returned to the Congo for a month for the making of a film about her life as a missionary doctor there, aimed at inspiring Christians to the missionary call. It was during that visit that God completed his healing of the trauma she received during the Simba Uprising in 1964, down to 'even a grain of bitterness'. *Digging Ditches*, page 152

[6] Later in her memoires, Mary Harrison wrote that Muriel was her greatly loved fellow worker, well educated, adventuresome, spiritually ahead of her in knowledge of the scriptures and her intimacy with the living Christ.

[7] Elisabethville was renamed Lubumbashi in 1966.

[8] David Davies, *With God in Congo Forests*, page 17

[9] David Davies, *The Captivity and Triumph of Winnie Davies*

[10] Helen Roseveare, *Living Stones*, page 79

[11] Winnie Davies was born in Wales. Today a memorial to her stands outside the church of St Tydfil's, in Coedpoeth, near Wrexham in northern Wales.

[12] David Davies, *With God in Congo Forests*, tells Idoti's story.

29

Ivor's Impact in New Zealand

Ivor's arrival in New Zealand had been timely for the nation's evangelical churches. A fresh spiritual awakening, the Charismatic Renewal, was about to take place, bringing many Christians into a new understanding and experience of the work of the Holy Spirit. The lessons Ivor and Rose learnt in the Congo revival proved important during the period of renewal.

It began unobtrusively in the early 1960s as Christians in mainline denominations experienced the baptism and gifts of the Holy Spirit. One of the catalysts for the renewal was the 1959 Billy Graham Crusade, when more than half a million people attended the six crusade meetings held in Christchurch, Wellington and Auckland. About 18,000 people stepped forward to commit or rededicate their lives to Christ. For the first time in New Zealand there was a widespread sense of unity among the mainline churches and Billy Graham was reported as saying he felt the country was on the verge of revival.

Ivor's addresses on revival during his first visit to New Zealand in 1957 had stirred listeners like Dorothy Leonard, who heard Ivor speak in Auckland. She was amazed. She went home and told her husband John she had listened to a man speak of things she had never heard before. Ivor was so aglow, so alight with the Spirit that she had a sense of revival flowing over the congregation in the telling of his story.

When Ivor and Rose later settled in New Zealand and assumed the WEC leadership they desired to see revival come to their adopted country. Ivor invited American revivalist preacher Leonard Ravenhill to speak at one of WEC's regular Saturday afternoon meetings and he had a profound effect on his audience, including Dale and David Garratt, founders of Scripture in Song. People caught the vision, attending meetings organised by Ivor specifically to pray for revival.

By 1963 Jim and Joy Dawson[1] held a prayer meeting every Friday evening in their home in Waikowhai, Auckland. The house group, which met together for more than three years, was unique at the time because it was interdenominational and open to whatever way God chose to move by his Holy Spirit. The gifts of the Spirit – prophecy, deliverance and discernment – operated freely. In addition there was much prayer for the nations and at times, a deep conviction of sin.

Some who joined the house group had belonged to Brethren assemblies, but when they received the baptism of the Holy Spirit they felt compelled by the hard-line views of their leaders to join more open-minded churches or groups like the Dawsons' group.

Most had received little teaching about the gifts of the Holy Spirit, often witnessing them before they understood what was happening. However, the Bible was always open and studied and the constant referral back to the Word gave a sense of safety, along with Ivor's gift of discernment to know what things were of God or of the flesh. It seemed to those present that they were in the school of the Holy Spirit, receiving his inspired leading and guiding.

Ivor continued to travel up and down New Zealand speaking at meetings, both on missionary themes and on revival. A number of Christians prayed for revival with expectation that the Lord would send it. They were grateful for Ivor's counsel, balanced approach and practical wisdom. His first-hand experience of the Congo revival was vital on occasions when difficulties arose.

For example, in 1964, a man appeared in Auckland, seemingly gifted in the word of knowledge and performing miracles and healings. While there appeared to be nothing wrong with his ministry some charismatic church leaders suffered attacks of depression after contact with him, and suspicion surfaced that he might be a false prophet. The man was invited to a meeting in the Dawsons' home and Arthur Wallis, a renewal leader, was given the responsibility of confronting him. The man quickly revealed his true colours. His face contorted. He swore and abused Arthur and then put a curse on him which left him completely unable to move.

Ivor ordered the man be removed from the meeting and joined other leaders to pray for Arthur. As they called on the Lord and resisted the attack of Satan in the name of Jesus the oppression lifted and Arthur moved freely again. The man departed from Auckland.

Near the end of 1970 Ivor was invited to take part in a march through central Auckland organised by Rob Wheeler, leader of the Auckland Christian Fellowship, in response to concern about the nation's moral decline. Marchers, carrying a large banner declaring Righteousness Exalts a Nation, sang their way to the Albert Park rotunda near the city centre. Not only did the march proclaim God's standards in the growing secular culture of the nation but it also marked greater co-operation between Pentecostal and evangelical Christians.

In early 1972 Ivor became chairman of the organising committee for a Jesus March. To prepare for the march they organised numerous prayer meetings, such as daily lunch-hour gatherings at the Baptist Tabernacle and half nights of prayer every Friday. In addition, hundreds of people gathered on Mt Eden at dawn each Sunday, overlooking the city and praying for it.

The committee was bursting with vision and drive, while Ivor gave wise and steadying leadership. Blyth Harper, the committee's administrator, and Muri Thompson were enthused at the mounting response from Christians across the city. They decided the impact of the march would be more dramatic if it started at 7.00 pm on a Friday late-shopping night. Without referring to the committee Muri and Blythe asked the mayor of Auckland to alter the city council permit to 7.00 pm from the stated 9.00 pm.

However, the committee had previously agreed to the later time. When Ivor heard of it he saw it as a breach of unity which could have had disastrous results. He had learned the importance of moving together in the unity of the Spirit in any work for God and insisted they keep to the time of 9.00 pm.

On 5 May 1972 more than 10,000 people marched down Queen Street, singing to the music of four Salvation Army bands and waving banners that praised the name of Jesus. After the exuberant crowd gathered outside the chief post office Ivor read a Charter for Righteousness which he presented to Sir Dove-Myer Robinson, the mayor of Auckland, and Muri Thompson followed, preaching a message of salvation. The rally's leader, David Jacobsen, then asked the crowd to support Muri in sending a request to the Prime Minister, John Marshall, to call the nation to a national day of prayer and fasting.

The Prime Minister said he would support such a day if church leaders took the initiative. However, when the proposal was put before a Wellington meeting of church leaders in August 1972 the consensus was that there was no serious need for such a day and churches were advised to pray for reconciliation on World Communion Sunday.

Nevertheless, the march had positive results. The Auckland march was the catalyst for other similar marches throughout the country. Blyth Harper and Ivor stood together on the steps of Parliament Building, marvelling how God had brought them to Wellington to share in the climax of the Jesus marches and to be a part of the present movement. The name of Jesus was proclaimed nationwide and barriers between church denominations were further removed, creating a degree of unity and love that remained into the future.

Ivor and Rose were very active in their local fellowship, Valley Road Baptist Church,[2] in which they were involved for more than 30 years. By 1979 the church supported a team of over twenty overseas missionaries, nearly half of which were linked with WEC, including two of Ivor and Rose's daughters and their husbands. Ivor was instrumental in keeping Valley Road Church on an even keel through the Charismatic Renewal, avoiding the excesses that damaged other churches, but at the same time encouraging people to lead a life guided by the Holy Spirit.

In his rich powerful wide-ranging voice Ivor often sang solo in meetings, choosing songs that had an impact. He spoke to the church several times about the life of holiness and the lessons learned from the Congo Revival. Even twenty years or more after the event his accounts never failed to have an impact on his audience. On one occasion, after Ivor finished his address during a Sunday service, the congregation sat in stunned silence for half an hour before anyone moved.

Ivor and Rose were active among the church's young people, regularly hosting at the WEC headquarters after-service singing and supper evenings, attended by 60 or more people. With their wise counsel they assisted many young Christians who later went on to make their mark in the nation. Ivor became the respected elder statesman of the church, both leaders and members of the congregation gravitating to him for advice long after he resigned from eldership in 1980.

Mike Pitama, a former gang leader who later worked successfully among the long-term unemployed, was a young person who, in the early 1980s, often visited the Davies. After Mike became a Christian Ivor offered to coach him as he struggled to study the Bible. For at least six months, Mike arrived outside their flat on his motorcycle about 4.00 pm, just after their afternoon nap.

Ivor and Mike started off with a karakia[3] before a Bible reading and some discussion, followed by homework for the following week.

From Mike's perspective it was man-to-man communication, sharing problems from work with an excellent listener. Rose always had muffins for them before Mike mounted his bike, grateful for Ivor's beneficial influence and aware that his love of rugby league could have easily drawn him away from the Word.

The New Zealand WEC work continued to grow, with missionary candidates increasing in numbers. By 1974 there were 65 New Zealanders abroad and five full-time home workers. Ivor and Rose made the many missionary candidates who passed through the headquarters feel part of one large family group.

Prayer always played a prominent role in the Davies' lives. They were dedicated intercession partners, a formidable force in prayer, with a lifelong pattern of morning devotions. After they retired each morning began with a 6.00am cup of tea, then prayers which covered the family, overseas missionaries, friends and even world leaders. Overnight guests in their small flat could not help but overhear the murmur of prayer from the elderly couple's bedroom in the early morning. Probably if they had listened closely they would have heard their own names mentioned, as the Davies prayed for virtually everyone they came in contact with.

In 1976 Ivor and Rose, at the age of 72, retired and passed the responsibilities of leadership over to a younger couple, Allan and Alison Shadbolt, who had worked with WEC in India.

[1] The Dawsons later became Youth with a Mission leaders in Los Angeles.

[2] It became Valley Road International Church some years later.

[3] Maori word meaning prayer or prayers.

30

Just a Man

The year 1985 was bitter-sweet, marked with sorrow and celebration. In mid-January Miriam, the family's eldest daughter, died of cancer at the age of 46 and later in the year Ivor and Rose celebrated their 50th wedding anniversary.

Miriam and her husband, Brian Woodford, were told of her illness the year before, just as they were to begin a new phase of outreach for WEC in the Philippines. After an operation they returned to New Zealand for Miriam to recuperate and she seemed to improve. But further X-rays revealed the spread of the cancer.

Ruth, and her husband Maurice, had returned to New Zealand from Singapore due to the failing health of Maurice's father. When Ioan from Canada and Evan from Tasmania arrived for Christmas all of Ivor and Rose's children, including Megan, were in the same place at the same time for the first time in 27 years.

Miriam's family and members of Valley Road Baptist Church began praying for her healing. But God had other plans and on 17 January she died at the WEC headquarters. Both Rose and Ivor were much affected by Miriam's early death. It came as Rose was battling with her own seriously deteriorating health and she felt keenly the injustice of her daughter dying at a relatively young age while she, her elderly mother, lived on.

Ivor was affected in a less obvious way. Miriam's death brought him face-to-face with his own mortality. He was now ageing, with his death not too far in the future, and he struggled with the prospect. Having preached and taught and encouraged others in their faith for many years he had to come to a new place of faith and peace for himself. As a young man in the Belgian Congo Ivor had been challenged many times to live what he preached but now in old age, regarded as a statesman of the church, he had to face his own personal inner challenge. He found great encouragement in the book *Dying to Live*, by Jim Graham, a Baptist minister in the United Kingdom.

Ivor and Rose's wedding anniversary celebration followed in September. Their far-flung family again flew into Auckland – Ioan from Canada, Evan and Jenny and their family from Tasmania, and Brian Woodford from England. An added surprise was the arrival from Britain of Eric and Daisy, Rose's sister, who had also worked in the Congo. It was the first time in more than 30 years that so many members of the extended family were together.

The week of celebration included a four-day family reunion at Willow Park Camp in Auckland and an evening of Congo and family reminiscences over a meal at a Chinese restaurant. Their church and other friends arranged another celebration attended by over 200 people and a special church service was based on God's goodness in marriage, with son Evan preaching and Ivor praying for all the married couples. Ruth and Maurice were then recommissioned for their WEC work in Singapore.

As family members departed Rose underwent a major medical examination. She had been unwell since the beginning of the year but rallied during Miriam's final weeks and the wedding anniversary celebrations. The checkup indicated that Rose was seriously ill with cancer.

She and Ivor shared the news with family and friends. Rose had always loved the Word of God. There had been hardly a dry eye among members of her church the morning she recited, word-perfect, Psalm 103. Again Rose recited the same psalm to her extended family a few days before she died. The last words of the psalm, 'Bless the Lord, O my soul', fittingly summed up her whole purpose in life.

Two days later Rose slipped into a coma. Blyth Harper, Ivor's close friend, sat and wept with him at Rose's bedside hours before she passed away, and in the early hours of Sunday 22 September she went to be with the Lord, eight months after her daughter Miriam and several weeks short of her 81st birthday. At the funeral the following Tuesday there were numerous moving tributes.

The timing of Rose's passing was a miracle, allowing the widely dispersed family to be together, leaving them with a fresh, happy, lasting memory of her. Though they were together for only a week, and in spite of her pain, Rose revelled in the experience of family closeness.

Ivor wept and grieved over Rose's departure but he experienced a tremendous encounter after her passing, assuring him that she was in the Lord's presence, free from suffering. Megan witnessed something of the event. She went looking for her father and found him in his bedroom, with his hands raised up to heaven and a wonderful expression of joy and adoration on his face. She turned to tiptoe out, for she knew she had just witnessed something private and holy. Her father caught sight of her and later told her that he was "having a glory time", which helped him to release Rose.

After her death Ivor continued to live in their flat on the grounds of the WEC headquarters, showing eager interest in new missionary candidates and their training. He participated in the regular prayer meetings and was always willing to receive into his home people needing counselling and prayer.

People arrived for a conversation and for prayer, to listen, to observe, and to try to imbibe something of the spirit of the man. They talked together of God's ways and purposes, discussing missions, countries, and God's hand in world events. Visitors were impressed with Ivor's extensive world view and wide interest, though he was in his senior years. Ivor was up-to-date and informed in his reading, knowing politically what was going on in different countries, even those that many had hardly heard of.

Ivor would pray passionately for world leaders, for political struggles in different countries and for their effect on the spread of the gospel. When visitors prayed together with Ivor for things close to his heart, like his family and missions, Ivor was always thankful, telling the Lord how much he loved him. When they began to praise and worship Ivor would rise up like a warrior to pray and intercede, his meekness part of his tremendous strength.

Ivor's church pastor, Dennis Grennell, was impressed with Ivor's humility before men much younger than himself, for he never lost sight of his humanity. He called Dennis to come and pray with him one day, saying he was having a battle with his thought life. Ivor was well into his eighties. Dennis was moved to think that the old saint was open enough to invite him to pray with him to gain victory.

Even as a senior citizen Ivor still thoroughly enjoyed singing. In 1987 he and Blyth Harper sang together in the choir of the Luis Palau Mission. Night after night they stood together, Ivor singing a deep rich bass, as only a Welsh man could.

Whether gathering in Wales or in New Zealand the family congregated around the piano to sing, joining in Welsh hymns and songs of the revival, easily and naturally breaking into parts. They so enjoyed blending their voices in *Ar Hyd Y Nos* (All through the night), and in *Guide me o thou great Jehovah* to the tune Cwm Rhondda, and in *Calon Lan* (A pure heart). Often the worship songs were in the minor key which the Welsh love, like *Oh the Deep, Deep Love of Jesus*. Ivor's children always enjoyed their father's wonderful solo voice even in his later years.

A highlight of Ivor's final year, eight months before his death, was the visit to Canada to his eldest son, Ioan, his wife Diane, of Jewish decent, and their family. Ivor had not previously met Ioan's two youngest sons, Justin and Benjamin, nor others of their extended family. The primary reason for the two-week visit was to witness the bar mitzvah of thirteen-year-old Justin.

Ivor asked his daughter Megan to accompany him. She was surprised he was so keen to make the arduous journey because he had been unwell. But Ivor had a wonderful time in Toronto where he met again Ioan's eldest son Eric, his wife Angela and their baby Oliver as well as Eric's brother Todd. He was very interested to meet Diane's father, Mr Bellam, a devout Jew, and had several stimulating discussions with him. Ivor had always been captivated by the Jewish people, their customs, and their place in biblical prophecy and found the bar mitzvah fascinating.

The ceremony became another family reunion when they were joined by Evan and Jenny, who were travelling through North America for WEC. Over the years Ioan had told his sons a great deal about Ivor and Rose but it was difficult for them to have an accurate image of them without meeting them in person. Now face to face Ivor made a great impression on his four grandsons.

Ivor's passing came suddenly on 8 July 1991, when he was almost 87 years old. There was no indication of anything seriously wrong with him until a few hours before his death. The day before he had attended the morning service at his local church, and spent the afternoon at Megan's home, before returning to the church for an evening video session. Ivor thoroughly enjoyed it, the first instalment of a documentary on recent archeological excavations in the Middle East. As a friend drove him home he mentioned how much he was looking forward to the sequel the following week.

Ivor went to bed, but phoned Megan three hours later, complaining of serious pains. Megan arrived quickly, wondering if his discomfort was the result of over-exertion in the garden the previous day. When she realised her father's problems were more severe she summoned a doctor who recommended immediate admission to hospital. The medical staff diagnosed a ruptured aortic aneurysm. His only chance of survival was an immediate operation. However, Ivor died under the anesthetic.

Though Ivor's death came as a shock to family and friends the way in which he died was a blessing. Megan and others who knew Ivor well agreed that he would not have made a good patient or coped well with a lingering death. For that reason Megan had often prayed that when her father died he would go quickly. Her prayer was indeed answered.

Ivor's thanksgiving memorial service four days later was a tremendously uplifting experience for the 300 people who attended. In the two-hour service family and friends listened as numerous people testified how their lives had been enriched by Ivor. One was Blyth Harper who spoke about something very close to Ivor's heart. He said he and Ivor seemed to be on the same wave length, drawn together by love for Jesus and a vision for revival. Ivor's life was never the same after his first-hand experience of the outpouring of the Holy Spirit in the Congo. What God had done there Ivor believed he could do again in New Zealand and across the world. The fire continued to burn, with the vision undimmed for the rest of his life, as he planted seeds of revival and prayed for it to come to pass.

A memorial service for Ivor was also held in Wales, with Ivor's three surviving brothers – Luther, Haydn, and David – among the many who attended. The brothers, more than anyone else, remembered the stark contrasts between the brother they knew in his youth and the man he became in adulthood. There was the sickly and frail boy who in later life battled the Congo jungles and addressed tens of thousands of people in public meetings. There was the shy youth and the disturbed teenager considering himself a failure who, years after his conversion, became a respected and loved leader to many and an elder statesman in the church. They also remembered the brother who maintained family unity by faithfully writing regularly to each one wherever he was at the time.

Ivor's sons and daughters wrote after his death, "We are an unusual family: in the end we are now British, Canadian, Australian, and New Zealand citizens. Over the years we have often had hurried times together – a fortnight here, a month there – and yet we were close, as though we had never been apart. The transparent reality of Dad's love for Jesus was obvious to us. We talked and laughed together, and thrilled to the stories of the Congo, of what God was doing in the world today, of Dad's latest prayer burden for Gadhafi, or someone else that he'd recently met in Auckland. Dad's prayer was positive and consistent and we felt the loss of it when he was gone. His Christianity was not the stuff of plaster saints but that of a real living person."

Ivor was asked once what sort of man Rees Howells was. With a smile and twinkle in his eye, he said, "Oh, he was just a man", and he left his hearers to make their own conclusions.

Perhaps Ivor would say similarly of himself, "Oh, I was just a man." But surely his life story speaks volumes to the calibre of that man and to the greatness of the God he served.

Appendix

Ivor and Rose's Family

One of the interesting features of the development of WEC was that the mission did not have in significant numbers many workers who were the adult children of former missionaries. Ivor and Rose's children were different, for three of their five children became full-time workers with WEC International – Miriam, Evan and Ruth.

Miriam was the second child and the eldest daughter in the family. Together with her brothers Ioan and Evan, she lived in the WEC Missionary Children's Home in Arbroath, Scotland, when their parents returned to work in the Congo in 1948, attending a local school. She trained as a nurse and midwife before attending the Bible College of Wales, Swansea, like her father. Joining her parents in New Zealand in 1965 she completed a missionary candidates' course and went to Upper Volta, now Burkina Faso. There she met and married missionary Brian Woodford. They later worked in Ghana and studied for several years in the United States, before lecturing at the Bible College of New Zealand, Miriam teaching Greek.

They had just begun a new work in the Philippines, recruiting nationals as workers for WEC, when Miriam was diagnosed with cancer. They returned to New Zealand where Miriam passed away in 1985. Brian remarried Lyn and they worked together in Africa and at WEC's International office before relocating to New Zealand where they taught at Eastwest College, the New Zealand Missionary Training College.

After working in New Zealand as a salesman Evan, the third child in the family, graduated from the WEC Missionary Training College in Tasmania and completed a candidates' course in Sydney. He married Jenny and they moved back to the college in Tasmania where he became a lecturer and later principal. In 1992 he and Jenny shifted to the UK as Deputy International Directors and from 1999 to 2004 they served as International Directors, travelling extensively in their leadership roles. They returned to live in Australia and Evan passed away in 2021.

Ruth, the youngest of the family and the only one born in Wales, trained as a nurse before attending the Bible College of New Zealand (now Laidlaw College) and completing a candidate's course. She married Maurice Charman who had been serving with WEC in Taiwan for seven years. With their church they ran a hostel outreach for international students in Auckland before moving to Singapore in 1980-88 to recruit workers. They then moved to Australia, pastoring a Chinese church for two years before joining the Worldview WEC Training College for twelve years. Back in New Zealand they served as directors of WEC NZ for six years, before shifting to Cambridge, then back to Auckland. They continue to work alongside WEC ministries, including IMM, a mobilising ministry which recruits new workers from non-traditional mission sending countries.

Like her older siblings Megan, the second youngest, was born in the Belgian Congo and spent her childhood there until she was eleven. After four years in Britain – one in Wales with the family, and three at The Elms in Scotland – she shifted with her parents and Evan and Ruth to Auckland where she trained in general nursing and midwifery. Over subsequent years she worked in hospitals overseas and in Auckland, including St Helen's Hospital and St Joseph's Mercy Hospice. Her experience in palliative care enabled her to look after Miriam and her parents in their final months before they passed away. She attended Valley Road Baptist Church and was involved in their ministries of Alpha and Cleansing Streams. More recently she moved to live with Ruth and Maurice as her own health deteriorated.

After completing his National Service in Britain Ioan, the eldest of the siblings, graduated from the London School of Economics, choosing a career in sociology. He taught at Essex University and married his first wife, Virginia. Later he became a professor of sociology at York University in Toronto, Canada, writing several books and marrying his second wife, Diane. Ioan spent less than ten years of his life living under the same roof as his parents, with his relationship to them largely based on correspondence. One of the reasons he became a writer was that all his life he was taught by his parents to be a writer – to express his feelings and to tell them what he was thinking, crucial if they were to continue as a family unit. He died in 2000.

The Davies truly became an international family, living at various times in North America, Africa, Australia, South East Asia and the South Pacific, but staying in contact through letters and emails and praying for each other.

Ioan's Words at His Father's Funeral

Ioan, who flew from Canada for his father's funeral, gave a perspective on his parents' life that few others would have experienced or seen. Ioan said: "The life of a missionary has particular types of pain. One of my parents' greatest senses of pain was that I never lived with them after I was very young. The last time I lived with my parents was when I was eight to nine years old. I had six months with them when I was eighteen, spent three weeks with them in New Zealand in 1980, and in November 1990, Dad spent two weeks in Toronto. It was painful for me and my children who had a grandfather and grandmother whom they could not meet.

"The cost to all of us of living great distances apart is that we have had to draw on all our internal resources to maintain family and maintain our own sense of ourselves. We have had to work at being a family in such circumstances.

"The reasons for being apart were not, in a sense, chosen. I don't believe my father would have known that when they left for the Congo in 1948 and left us three children in Scotland, that when they returned, I would be called up into the army, making it difficult for me to stay with them. And at the end of that I would go to university and they would be called here to New Zealand. These fractures have not been chosen by either side.

"I'm so grateful that Dad and Mum found it absolutely crucially important that, by hook or by crook, our relationship would go on. And when their letters came they were filled with good humour, vivid description, and long accounts of their activities, so I had a continued sense of what they were doing and they didn't slip away. So when we met again, we were able to pick up where we left off."

Bibliography

Benge, Janet & Geoff, *Norman Grubb: Mission Builder*, YWAM Publishing, 2019

Davies, David M, *With God in Congo Forests*, WEC, 1971

Davies, Evan, *Whatever happened to CT Studd's mission? Lessons from the history of WEC International*, WEC Publications, 2012

Evans, Eifion, *The Welsh Revival of 1904*, Evangelical Press, 1969

Grubb, Norman, *After C. T. Studd*, Lutterworth Press, 1955

Grubb, Norman, *C. T. Studd, Cricketer and Pioneer*, Lutterworth Press, 1978

Grubb, Norman, *Mighty Through God: the life of Edith Moules*, Lutterworth Press, 1951

Grubb, Norman, *Rees Howells Intercessor*, Lutterworth Press, 1981

Grubb, Norman, *Successor to C. T. Studd: The Story of Jack Harrison*, Lutterworth Press, 1950

Ed. Grubb, Norman, *This is That: The Spirit of Revival – A First Hand Account of the Congo Revival of the 1950s*, Christian Focus, 1954. Reissued in 2000 with a new introduction by Helen Roseveare

Harrison, Mary, *Mama Harri – And No Nonsense*, Oliphants, 1969

Moules, Len, *This is No Accident: Testimonies of a Trial of Faith in Congo*, 1964

Penn-Lewis, Jessie, *The Awakening of Wales*, The Overcomer Literature Trust

Roseveare, Helen, *Digging Ditches: The Last Chapter of an Inspirational Life*, Christian Focus, 2005

Roseveare, Helen, *Give Me This Mountain*, Inter-Varsity Fellowship, 1966

Roseveare, Helen, *Living Stones: Seventy-five Years of WEC International,* WECPublications, 1988

Searle, Charlie, *God Can*, about 1950

Stewart, James, *Invasion of Wales by the Spirit through Evan Roberts*, Christian Literature Crusade, 1970

Vincent, Eileen, *CT Studd and Priscilla*, WEC Publications, 1988

Whittaker, Colin, *Great Revivals*, Marshalls Paperbacks, 1984

Digital

A Diary of Revival: the story of the 1904 Welsh Awakening, Vision Video https://www.youtube.com/watch?v=5M8Fala4o-E

Mama Luka Comes Home – Cross TV – www.cross.tv/78482

1953 Congo Revival, https://romans1015.com/1953-congo/